The Vintage Years

THE STORY OF HIGH TOR VINEYARDS

Everett Crosby

HARPER & ROW, PUBLISHERS
New York, Evanston, San Francisco, London

Illustrations follow page 120.

FIRST EDITION

Designed by Patricia G. Dunbar

Library of Congress Cataloging in Publication Data

Crosby, Everett.
  The vintage years.
  1. Crosby, Everett. 2. High Tor Vineyards.
I. Title.
TP547.C76A33   338.7′66′3200924 [B]   72-9113
ISBN 0-06-010924-6

PROLOGUE

Originally this was a cartoon, a copy of which was given me by a friend who realized all too well the basic truths involved. An old German winemaker on his deathbed imparts his final piece of wisdom to his sons: "One can also make wine from grapes." Obviously none of the sons believes him. They stare at the dying man coldly, fully convinced that he is going to his grave with his secrets intact, that they will never be able to match the wine of the father, who will so soon be heavenly. The missing chemical, the vital adulterant, he has kept to himself. *Grapes,* indeed!

Far-fetched? Consider a partial listing of the materials authorized for treatment of wine in Part 240 of Title 26, Code of Federal Regulations: acetic acid, Actiferm, activated carbon, Aferrin, AMA, Antifoam "A", ascorbic acid, Atmos 300, bentonite, bone charcoal, calcium carbonate, calcium sulfate, carbon, carbon dioxide, casein, citric acid, combustion product gas, copper sulfate, Cufex, diammonium phosphate, diethyl pyrocarbonate, Fulgur, fumaric acid, glycine, gum arabic, hydrogen peroxide, lactic acid, malic acid, mineral oil, nitrogen gas, pectolytic enzymes, phosphates, polyvinylpyrrolidone, potassium metabisulfite, Promine-D, Protovac PV-7916, Roviferm, sodium bisulfite, sodium carbonate, sodium caseinate, sodium metabisulfite, sorbic acid, Sparkaloid, sulfur dioxide, sulfuric acid, Takamine Cellulase 4,000, tannin, tartaric acid, Uni-Loid Type 43B, urea, Veltol and Yeastex.

Grapes? Well, they *are* mentioned. Subpart P, Production and Treatment of Natural Grape Wine: "Natural Grape Wine is the product of the juice of sound, ripe grapes [so far so good], made with cellar treatment authorized by this part . . ." and there the whole thing blows apart, because this authorized treatment consists in part of the materials listed above. Don't think you're going to do any better drinking French or German wines, for spray materials and chemical additives have been cleared for use there that have not and perhaps never will be cleared here. What to do? Well, there are a few who believe that wine is the product of the juice of sound, ripe grapes, period. I am one of those who so believe, and for twenty-two years my wife and I operated a bandbox winery named High Tor Vineyards in New York State's Hudson River Valley. And during those twenty-two years, only one of the materials listed above ever went into our wines, and that is a material which I will mention later and which has been in use since the days of Pasteur.

The Vintage Years

Last words of the little old German winemaker to his sons, desperate to learn his secret for making good wine: "One can also make wine from grapes."

Verlag A. Hurtes, Münstereifel.   Bernhard Göffels pinx.

Das Geheimnis des alten Weinhandlers,
sein letztes Vermächtnis an seine Söhne:
„Mer kann och uss Druve Wing mache".

I can so clearly remember my youth in California, in what I now think back on as the golden age of prohibition. Good wine, honest wine, was seventy-five cents a gallon, and you could never leave with your jug until you had drunk at least a jelly glass drawn straight from the barrel by your friendly neighborhood bootlegger. Except that they never thought of themselves as bootleggers. They were winemakers, on whom fate and the ghastly puritanical ethic of America had played an outrageous trick. They cared about wine, they took pride in their wine, and once having made such a delectable product they considered it the height of folly not to sell it.

At that time I was going to San Ramon Valley Union High School, over a range of low hills from the Bay of San Francisco. Somewhat to the south was Livermore, one of the great wine districts of America, and we used to play basketball against Livermore High School. But more often we played another school in that same Livermore Valley, Amador Valley Joint Union High School, and when the two teams took the floor— ours with SRVUHS emblazoned across our not too mountainous chests and theirs with AVJUHS—you couldn't see the ball for the letters. But Amador Valley High was located in Pleasanton, and what made this town memorable was the fact that the local speakeasy was directly across the street from city hall, and the mayor and his aides could often be seen through the wide-open and unshuttered windows standing at the bar, drinking the illegal but good red wine of the country. The white wine then left much to be desired, and though better than forty years of honest work and experimentation have gone into the problem, no California white wine yet can measure up to the best of the reds.

After a game in Pleasanton our team always stopped in at this speakeasy for a jelly glass of wine. Of course we were too young, but as it was illegal to sell wine to anyone, this sticky issue was never raised. After the glass was downed we would buy a gallon in our own jug, which we always carried for this purpose, along with two or three loaves of sour Italian bread. We would pile into the topless roadster, complete with rumble seat, and pass the jug around, slowing down its action with huge chunks of bread torn from a still warm loaf. Down the road, we went past the whorehouse at Santa Rita, which an occasional team member patronized from time to time. But never on game night, for everyone saved his strength for the game, and everyone was too tired afterward. Never, it must be added, by your humble servant, for my mother had instilled such a fear of VD in me that I would not even accept a cigarette from anyone who had recently been inside that palace of pleasure.

On the threshold of maturity, speeding along under the stars, the pear and walnut trees sliding by, the brooding bulk of Mount Diablo looming to the east . . . and people ask me why I have had such a romance with wine. My only answer is, "Why didn't all the others in the car?"

For make no mistake. An association with the grape is a romance. The grape must be courted like a woman, and it is for this reason that most winemakers believe passionately in their own product. More than any other food—and it is a food—wine reflects the taste of its maker. If he has bad taste he obviously doesn't know it and would refuse to believe it. This is not true of the makers of Blunder Bread, or of process cheese. They *know* their products are lousy and on all but the most public occasions they eat *real* bread and *real* cheese.

Not so the winemaker. He drinks his product, and he drinks it daily. I once knew a man who operated a tiny winery and tried to compete with the giants by putting out wine of the same quality at a lower price. In vain I tried to tell him that the only way a small man could exist was to make a better wine than the giants could afford to, and to charge accordingly. But he would take a loving sip and say, "It's as good as Petri, and it's cheaper. Why don't people buy it?" It was indeed as good as Petri. What it lacked was the multimillion-dollar advertising budget that made people remember Petri when they went to buy wine. Walking into a store in search of honest, inexpensive wine, a person would have no way of knowing that my friend's product was actually as good as Petri and a few cents cheaper. So they bought the wine that was familiar, and after developing a bitter hatred of the general public my friend went out of business, still trying to undercut Petri, Roma and Gallo.

The reason a small man can make a better wine than the giants is very simple. Wine is a matter of taste, and a small man can make a wine exactly to his taste; if his taste is good he will find enough people who agree with him to sell out his limited production. But the giants must sell to a mass market of undefined tastes. There must be compromise everywhere. A major error in judgment would be disastrous, for if a winery were stuck with millions of cases of unsold wine, bankruptcy would follow swiftly. A small winery can improve its products through experimentation, and if an occasional barrel is lost it can always be dumped and no real harm has been done. Further, sheer bulk alone retards quality. Given equal grapes and adequate equipment, the same knowledgeable man can always make a thousand gallons better than he can make a million.

My early love for wine was an unlikely affair for, born into a family that looked down on wine, I spent my first years in Piedmont, California, in those days the capital of WASPdom. Wine was confined to the lower classes, and the feeling in Piedmont was that only members of the naturally criminal element drank it. Actually it was not criminal for the head of a family to make up to two hundred gallons a year provided it was not sold or transported in any way. But law enforcement agents generally looked the other way if nothing stronger than table wine was involved and a regular river of wine flowed through the grape-growing country. Suddenly, when I was sixteen, we moved to what was then at least marginally grape-growing country, Walnut Creek. Today it is a teeming metropolis, but then it was too small to have its own high school, and I elected to go to the one at Danville, six miles to the south. Hence the rivalry with the schools in the nearby *real wine* country, and the scene that opened this book—the beginning of my unlikely affair.

When I was eighteen my mother in her wisdom sent me for an entire summer alone in Europe. I crossed over on the *Aquitania* in June of 1929, a few short months before the whirlwind struck. It was a gay trip, and everyone danced much as they danced before Waterloo. I did not know the name of a single wine, other than "red" or "white." Sherry I had read about, however, and I ordered a bottle of it from the bar and drank a considerable amount in my cabin the second night out. I had one of my more memorable hangovers the next morning, and learned lesson number one. When approaching a fortified wine, a wine to which brandy has been added, treat it with extreme respect.

The summer was spent in Paris, Zurich, Berlin and Wiesbaden, where I discovered for the first time the glories of

German wine. Then on to Rotterdam, Antwerp, Seville and Barcelona, where a friendly Swiss hotel clerk gave me a two-week course in the basics of wine and wine drinking, and where I also discovered shellfish cookery and saffron, to which I am addicted to this day. Then Milan and Genoa, and the boat for home. And it was on this ship, the *Conte Grande,* that word of the stock market's Black Tuesday reached us by radio, just as we were passing the Azores. People still danced, but not as gaily.

By now I had tasted *wine,* the best that Europe had to offer, and to my unsophisticated taste, at least, the wines made by my California neighbors in their cellars did not stack up too badly. Incidentally, I think that most of the gallon wines made in California today are a great deal better than the average French *vin ordinaire,* and are a much better buy than most of the cheap foreign wines that now flood the country.

It was a touch difficult to return to San Ramon Valley Union High School after viewing the wonders of the world, but as I still had one year to go, return I must. There was, however, a mitigating factor that took out some of the sting, for about a year earlier a friend had asked me to go to the fourteenth-birthday party of a girl I didn't know, a girl with the unlikely name of Alma Bridget Cross, a girl I resolved to know better someday. The following fall she entered high school and I kept her under close observation. Shortly before debarking for Europe I had pulled off one of the most complicated shuffles in the history of juvenile perfidy and left my best friend stuck with my cast-off girl while I latched on to Alma. So now, if the shuffle hadn't come unstuck in the meantime, I had that to look forward to.

It hadn't, and after I had driven her to school for a week or so (I had to pass her house), she noticed the unappetizing lunch I carried. My mother never cared the slightest for food, and allowed the cook to put whatever she felt like in my lunchbox, with the result that it was generally a dry slab of cheddar cheese between two thick slices of unbuttered bread. Alma suggested that she make enough lunch for two, and the adage about the way to a man's heart was never so truly proved.

I had determined to be a singer, and with that in mind decided to study music. But I had always been interested in science, particularly physics, and shortly before my graduation from high school, on a sudden whim I entered a statewide competition for a scholarship to Harvard in optical physics. To everyone's surprise—mine most of all—I finished first and was offered the scholarship. But then my mother got into the act and said I could not accept it. She had plenty of money to send me independently, and if I took the scholarship I would deprive some boy who perhaps couldn't afford to go otherwise. I wrestled with this one for days. I would have liked to go as the winner of a scholarship, but my interest in optical physics wasn't enough for me to go as just another student, with Mother footing the bills. It is interesting to speculate what might have happened, for even without this training I invented an all-electronic system of color television, for which I was granted a patent in 1942.

Having made my decision, I enrolled in the University of Southern California, which then had the best school of music on the Coast. Once a month I flew north to see Alma in a Ford-Stout trimotor plane, better known as the "Tin Goose." On one of these flights during my second year at college, the metal strip came off one of the wooden propellers and that motor had to be shut down. Much was made of the fact that these planes could fly with only two engines, but nevertheless we lost altitude steadily and by the time we got to San Jose we could easily read the road signs. We were about fifty feet off the ground when we got to the airport.

This unnerved Alma considerably, and when I came home for Christmas vacation that year we got married, even though she still had six months of high school to complete, which she did when an understanding principal let her send in the work by mail. A funny sidelight to our wedding came about when we went to the county office building in Martinez to get our wedding license. We were both under age, Alma seventeen and I twenty, so her father and my mother went along to give their consent. The clerk thought that it was the two older people who wanted the license and had it half made out in their names before the error was discovered. There were many who said we were too young, but I am happy to say that after forty years we are still together, due no doubt to the many and varied benefits of the grape.

All this was during the worst years of the Depression. Everything was incredibly cheap, including wine, and as the economy worsened more and more people gave up spirits and turned to wine. I believe it is safe to say that during the last years of prohibition, the annual per capita consumption of table wine was the highest it has ever been in the history of the United States. Certainly vastly more than the just shy of two gallons a year average drunk by every American today.

In addition to being able to buy wine on almost any street corner, you could make it right in your apartment with the Wine Brick. This was the brainchild of one Mabel Walker Willebrant, one of the first women to hold high political office in this country. After heading the department that enforced prohibition for some years, she turned her considerable talents to getting around the law that by now she knew so well. She resigned her post and managed a private company that brought out a pressed brick containing all the necessary ingredients of wine—grape concentrate, sugar, acid and dried yeast. All it lacked was water and know-how. As it was illegal to impart the know-how directly, the brick contained instructions which said: "Do not immerse this brick in five gallons of warm water, for this will cause it to ferment and turn into wine. But if this unfortunately happens under no circumstances siphon it into a clean jug after fermentation has stopped. But if as a result of accident this should happen care should be taken not to bottle and cap it, for this is illegal." Need I add that it made the lady and her backers a great deal of money?

Then suddenly what was always referred to as the "Noble Experiment"—at first seriously by its perpetrators, the Women's Christian Temperance Union, and later derisively by everyone else—ended. The abandoned wineries were cleaned and refitted, and vast new ones were built. The only slight problem was that the superior types of wine grapes shipped badly, and had all been pulled up to be replaced by varieties that would stand the long trip in a freight car to the eastern markets. I hardly need to say that toughness and quality seldom go hand in hand, with the result that when the great drought was over there were almost no top quality grape varieties left in California. Added to this, everyone was in a huge hurry to get on the market first, so that many shortcuts were taken and many questionable practices indulged in. As a result, the first legal wine left a great deal to be desired, and it turned a great many people off California wines for a good many years. I was among them.

Meanwhile the winemakers began the long process of rebuilding after the first tragic rush. But the damage was done, and the general public refused to believe that Calfornia wine was getting better year by year. What saved the business was World War II, and if ever the expression about an ill wind was valid it was in this case for the California winemakers. French wines, German wines, Italian wines disappeared one by one from the market, until there were only California wines left, plus a smattering of New York wines made from a different grape, a matter I will go into later. Alma and I were living by then in an apartment on East Seventy-third Street in New York. There was a wine store a block or so away run by a Frenchman, and when the last French bottle went he sadly suggested that we buy some from California. With some trepidation we tried the wines of Wente Brothers, from my old Livermore Valley neighborhood; then those of Louis Martini, Beaulieu, Inglenook. We were amazed at the quality, and realized that as a result of the first fiasco seven or eight years earlier we had turned into two of those most insufferable people, Imported Wine Snobs. I must report that even today millions of Americans suffer from this dreadful disease.

Also in the neighborhood was a small Viennese restaurant at which we frequently ate, which stocked several of Widmer's New York State white wines. Giddy from our success with the California wines, we threw discretion to the winds and ordered a bottle one night, and a whole new way of life opened up before us. For though it tasted different from any wine I had ever drunk, it was also extremely good, with a clean acidity that I had found missing in the California whites, and that made it go superbly well with some of the Viennese dishes.

It was now the early spring of 1941, and when the penthouse of the apartment house in which we were living became available at an absurdly low rental, we took it. We took it for two reasons, the first being that we had been married for almost ten years, and it seemed high time to consider starting a family. The second reason was that it would give us an opportunity to indulge in a limited way our joint passion for gardening. And among the things we wanted to grow were a couple of grapevines. The needle that had fluctuated for so long was beginning at last to swing toward true north.

Alma, efficient as ever, fulfilled the first of our goals by becoming pregnant within two months of moving into our spacious quarters. The second we took care of by ordering two "bearing age" Concord grapevines from a mail order nursery, which we planted in butter tubs on either side of the main doors leading out from the living room. Of course we should never have ordered "bearing age" anything, particularly grapevines,

9

for they are generally culls that have been hanging around in some neglected corner of the nursery in the hope that some sucker can be conned into taking them. One should never buy anything but sturdy one-year-old vines, but this we did not know.

In any case, the gangling, almost six-foot-tall plants thrived and showed every indication of being at home on the fourteenth floor of a Manhattan penthouse. Other things did well too, and we had floribunda roses, wisteria, bittersweet, Russian olive, an espalier apple tree, gladiolus, canna lilies and, a year or two later, a small vegetable garden from which we harvested tomatoes, scallions and lettuce.

Alma continued to be efficient, and deciding that seven and a half months was long enough to carry a baby, presented us on January fourteenth of the next year with a tiny but extraordinarily vociferous daughter, the only child, as it turned out, that we were to have. We were impossible parents, boiling, scrubbing and sterilizing everything. I suppose this was also a portent of things to come, for if one is not almost a monomaniac on absolute cleanliness one will never make really good white wine. Anyone can make red wine, clean, dirty or otherwise. But with white, there must simply be no chance of contamination, and it has been said that a bright, pale, absolutely clear white wine is the ultimate of the winemaker's skill.

We named our daughter Averil, after one of the earliest poems of the English language, which begins, "Between Mershe and Averil, when Spring beginneth to spray . . ." Our anticontamination policy was taken to the point of getting the superintendent to remove the bedroom door and replace it with a glass one, so that when friends came to admire the new arrival they could look through the pane without imparting any germs.

In March we decided to christen her, and we asked our good friends Ed and Connie Bayuk to be the godparents. The fact that Eddie was Jewish never entered our minds as a potential stumbling block, but we had not correctly calculated the bigotry of the times. Today I am sure it would be different, but in 1942 not a single Protestant church in New York would christen a child who had a Jewish godfather. In desperation we turned to a classmate of my father's, a man who had been his friend at Harvard, Reverend Laurence Hayward, minister of the Unitarian church at Newburyport, Massachusetts. He was delighted with the idea, saying that his church had no quarrel with Judaism. But he would have to get permission from his superiors. We supposed it was permission to perform a christening outside his own district. The hilarious thing was that he had to get permission to perform a christening, period. In our innocence we did not know that Unitarians do not necessarily accept the divinity of Jesus, and a full-fledged christening service was definitely not within the scope of their beliefs.

He got the permission, and a madder christening it is hard to imagine, a christening with half the guests Jewish, and with a Unitarian minister putting on a full Trinitarian service by blessing the holy water and naming the child "in the name of the Son and of the Father and of the Holy Ghost." To cap it all, we had decided to give our daughter my mother's name, Idolene, as her second name, but when Connie Bayuk got to that part she pronounced it "Idoline." Reverend Hayward knew my mother's name as well as he knew his own; he had in fact discussed marriage with her after she and my father were divorced. But with a perfectly straight face he said, "I name thee Averil Idoline Crosby."

Two things happened that summer of 1942: The grapevines flowered, one setting two bunches, and the other, one. And, in August, I went to work for the Voice of America. It was a demanding six-day-a-week job, with long hours, for lunch didn't count on government service in those days, and an eight-hour day meant from nine to six. This left me little time for outside affairs, and Alma, with the new baby on her hands, had even less. But I was determined to find out more about New York State wines and I read what I could and drank what I could. It was then we both discovered that if much of the New York white was excellent, the red was terrible beyond belief. Poking into the reasons for this, we found that while white varieties are by and large adapted to cold temperatures, there were then almost no red wine varieties that would stand the rigorous climate of New York, and winemakers relied heavily on the Concord for their red wines. Now the Concord is a most pleasant grape to eat, and it makes a fine jelly. But anyone who has developed a taste for the good vintages of Europe and California simply abhors its presence in a glass of wine.

Hearing of my interest, a fellow enthusiast gave me a copy of *Grapes of New York,* by the late Dr. Ulysses P. Hedrick, considered then to be the bible of eastern grape growing. This book, which first explained the special problems faced by the eastern vineyardist, hooked me on winemaking. It also gave me the desire to own a small vineyard someday, perhaps an acre or two where I could make a few gallons on a purely amateur basis. That day, of course, was still distant, and in the meantime our Concords on the terrace were ripening nicely. On a day in late September we held a vintage party, and although we didn't suspect it at the time, it was the precursor of many to come. The three bunches were picked and handed grape by grape to the guests, while New York State champagne was lifted in toasts.

Obviously the wine bug had bitten deeply, something I have seen again and again in others. A true wine buff will arrive at High Tor Vineyards, in Rockland County, and after he has looked around a stunned expression will spread slowly over his face as though he were being injected with Pentothal. Ninety percent of the time he will end up trying to buy the place even if he doesn't have the money, and knows he hasn't the money. This was beginning to happen to me on Seventy-third Street.

The net that was to gather me in to High Tor was tightening perceptibly.

In 1947 exit from this net was all but closed off when my wife and I bought a run-down Victorian house in West Nyack, Rockland County, New York, about seven miles from what was later to become High Tor Vineyards. One of the reasons we bought this house was a three-acre field across the brook that went with it. A vineyard, of course. And here we made mistake number one, the first of the many mistakes everyone must make when traveling the road from neophyte to professional winemaker. Happily I made most of mine as an amateur, but I must admit I made my share after the winery was bonded and we were in business.

What was this first mistake? It was simply that grapes cannot tolerate "wet feet," and this charming three-acre pasture was literally alive with springs. Also, it was at the bottom of a small valley where frosts hit early and hard. But in our enthusiasm we ordered 175 grapevines, hired a local farmer to plow part of the field, and in the spring of 1948 Alma and I, in hip boots, planted the vines ourselves.

Mistake number two was that we had not done our homework sufficiently. We read a standard book on grape varieties, and accepting it as gospel, we ordered such vines as Ontario, Sheridan, Westfield—all improved New York grape varieties. What we did not know, and should have, was that during the long years of prohibition no government money could be spent on grape experimentation if the variety under study was a wine grape. So all the research went into table varieties, which almost without exception made lousy wines. But experimentation had not stopped in Europe, and a fantastic group of new wine varieties were making their appearance under the loose category of "Franco-American Hybrids." These we knew nothing about. It is significant that twenty-four years later not one of the vari-

13

eties we bought, which were then the best that a leading New York State nursery had to offer, would now be even considered for the establishing of a new vineyard.

What is a grape hybrid? I am afraid, at the risk of boring any truly knowledgeable wine buff, that I must launch into an explanation that is repeated ad nauseam in every treatise on winegrowing—the "Story of Phylloxera." To begin with, all the grapes of Europe, in their thousands of varieties, are members of one species, *Vitis vinifera*. In North America there are over twenty species. The number varies depending upon which of the experts one reads. Until about 20 years ago the most widely used species in winemaking in eastern America was *Vitis labrusca,* whose definitive variety is Concord. I need say no more to a true wine lover to convince him that *Vitis labrusca* alone cannot make a drinkable wine. The next obvious question is "So why not plant *Vitis vinifera* in New York?" and this is where we come to phylloxera, a louse that feeds on the roots of grapevines. This pest was unknown in Europe and for many years in California, but it abounds in almost every square foot of soil in the East. Because of its existence the native wild grapes had to adapt to it, and developed root systems more or less impervious to its attacks. Not so the *vinifera* with its soft, pulpy root, so that every attempt to introduce it into America failed from the days of Sir Walter Raleigh—to the blank bewilderment of the settlers, who knew nothing of this tiny predator lurking just below the surface. Hops grew well, however, grain grew well, and so our ancestors gave up on wine and turned us into a beer and whiskey drinking nation long before phylloxera had been isolated and understood.

Man can never leave well enough alone, and some French enthusiast decided to see how American grapes would do in France. They did extremely well, practically wiping out the vineyards of France, Germany and Italy. For on the roots of

14

these vines a quantity of *Phylloxera vastatrix* were waiting for the moment to invade virgin soil, and the moment arrived. Starting in the early 1870s, this little louse raced through France, across the Rhine into Germany, down the Rhone Valley and across Provence to Italy, leaving devastation in its wake. Within five years of its introduction the great bulk of Europe's vineyards were well on their way to destruction, and only the Pyrenees and the relative isolation of the country prevented it from getting into Spain.

Naturally the enthusiast who caused the debacle had no idea what he was doing, for the true nature of the disease was just then beginning to be understood. I suppose the same thing could be said of the Ohio furniture manufacturer who had no way of knowing that the decorative elm wood boles he imported from Holland to his factory contained beetles carrying the lethal Dutch elm blight that wiped out the American elm over the past thirty or forty years.

One can only imagine the state of mind of the French nation, suddenly faced with the possibility of life without wine. *In extremis,* some even planted Concords, saying, "Alas, this is the only wine my children will know. It's better than nothing, but not much better."

But America, which gave every grape plague then known to the previously disease-free vineyards of Europe, also came to the rescue. It was by now known that the roots of native American grapes could resist phylloxera; it was widely believed, however, that any variety grafted onto such a root would inexorably turn into a vine that bore American fruit, a theory that happily turned out to be totally false. In the late 1870s and early '80s a few of the more daring French vineyardists began trying such grafts, and to everyone's amazement the resulting grapes were not only as good as the original parent growing on its own roots, but the new root had in many cases added an extra vigor to the resulting vine. So the French set about the laborious process of replanting all their classic varieties grafted onto New York roots, a situation that still obtains today.

But now a new problem was encountered. Many of their best previous varieties had been almost totally destroyed, and they had to turn to California to get grafting wood of these varieties. Thus it is that most of the great French vineyards were replanted with fruiting wood from California, grafted onto New York State roots. Unfortunately, during this interchange phylloxera continued its destructive march, going from New York to France, and from France to California, where the whole French experience was replayed.

How did the great French varieties get to California in the first place? Well, a certain Hungarian, Count or Colonel (he alternated the titles depending on the occasion) Ágoston Haraszthy, arrived in California in the early 1850s. He had tried to found a free-love colony in of all places Sauk City, Wisconsin. When it became apparent what he was up to, the righteous element in town lost no time in giving him the bum's rush, and accompanied by his four sons, Attila, Árpád, Béla and Géza, he tried again in San Diego. That city was not yet ready for what he had in mind, although a hundred years later he might have succeeded, and he moved on to found a vineyard, first at San Mateo and later at Sonoma, California. Apparently wine was more profitable and less controversial than his first love, and by 1861 he was important enough to have himself appointed chairman of the State Viticultural Commission. This was only eleven years after California became a state, and brings to mind a piece of doggerel known to the Native Sons of the Golden West.

> The miners came in forty-nine,
> The whores in fifty-one,
> And when they got together
> They produced the native son.

Eighteen fifty was the magic year in between these two great events, and that was the year California joined the union. I can't get over the feeling that somehow this says something about my native state.

Anyway, Count/Colonel Haraszthy went to Europe, paying his own way on the promise that he would be repaid by the legislature. And then an amazing thing happened: he did just what he had promised to do. (There is something ennobling about the grape that seems to bring out the best in a man, free-love advocate or no.) Two hundred thousand grape cuttings duly arrived in California, all labeled and catalogued. To cap it all, most of them rooted in the hospitable soil of California, and from them came almost all of the major wine species grown in the state today. An interesting sidelight, possibly apocryphal, is the story that one name had been hastily scribbled on a bundle of cuttings, and Haraszthy for the life of him couldn't read it on his return. Nor could he remember where he got it, and so the scribble was transcribed as "Zinfandel," which today is the mystery grape of California.

But Haraszthy could never settle down to the life of a wine-maker and businessman and so, perhaps dreaming of his earlier venture, he went out once more to conquer new territory, leaving the vineyards in the hands of Attila, Árpád, Béla and Géza. Somewhere in the jungles of Central America he died, probably as the result of a fever. But there is one version of his ending that I like to think fulfilled the romantic promise of the man. In it he is eaten by a crocodile. Incidentally, he never got back a nickel of the twelve thousand dollars he spent to make California one of the great wine areas of the world. It simply had to be a crocodile.

Grafting is an expensive and time-consuming business, and around the turn of the century certain European horticulturalists began the complicated process of crossing the American with the European species in an attempt to create new varieties with the disease resistance of the one and the grape quality of the other. It was a tedious business, but in the three-quarters of a century that have elapsed some remarkable varieties have emerged, almost totally immune to phylloxera and with a grape quality that in some instances is superior to certain of the older European standards. As an added dividend many had an increased winter hardiness that opened up whole new sections of the United States to viticulture. With the repeal of prohibition New York could once again turn to wine-grape experimentation, using the work of the French pioneers in this field as a guide. Promising new varieties began to appear and are still evolving to this day. The same situation exists in Canada, where enormous progress has been made in developing phylloxera-resistant and winter-hardy strains.

All of this, however, was unknown to the Crosbys in 1948, and we sloshed about our wet vineyard and wondered at the poor results. For when the skimpy vines began at last to bear grapes, the resulting wine left a great deal to be desired. As by now I knew that the location was about as bad as it could have been, I put all of the faults of the wine down to this.

These first years at West Nyack were happy and productive ones. I was writing several radio dramatic programs, one on a full-time basis and others part-time, and I need not point out that life is always easier when the money is rolling in. But I itched to get on with the winemaking, and while waiting for our own wet vines to make a better showing I began buying several boxes of California grapes from a Nyack fruit wholesaler and making wine from them, the first wine, incidentally, that I had ever made. The variety I bought was a red one named Carignane, which if well handled produces a light but quite drinkable wine. We invited our neighbors in to help us remove the grapes from the stems, a necessity when working with all but the highest-quality varieties, and perhaps a necessity even then. Thus we all sat around on the lawn, putting the stemmed

18

grapes into a large stone crock and partaking generously of inexpensive table wine from a jug. We toyed briefly with the idea of having some maidens tread out the juice with their feet, but outside of the very young, whose feet were too small, it was difficult to tell the maidens from the others, so we crushed them with a prosaic hand-cranked crusher borrowed from the friend who had given me Hedrick's book.

Making wine at home this way is perfectly legal, although technically you are supposed to write to the Alcohol, Tobacco Tax and Firearms Division of the Internal Revenue Service for permission. To my knowledge, no one has done this for years even though the permit is free, and when I once did so the startled inspector said it was the first one he had ever seen in his life. The requirements for this are rather strange. You may make no more than two hundred gallons in a single year, and you may not sell any of it. Further, you may not take it off the property or even give it away. Only the head of a family may get this permission, and you may not make the wine in company with your brother-in-law or uncle to be shared. Since a bachelor has no family to head, he is not allowed to make any. But the crusher in this department came a year or so ago when a wife asked for permission to make some wine for her family. She was refused, because she was not the head of the family. If her husband requested permission, that would be all right, but he was not in the least interested in making wine, which after all was his wife's hobby. Sorry, said the Internal Revenue Service; in our book only the husband is the head of a family, and your request is denied. I imagine that Betty Friedan and Bella Abzug have already mounted the barricades over this one.

Though I am a firm believer in following directions to the letter and to the comma, and though I had a copy of Phillip Wagner's book on home winemaking, than which there is no better, the quality of the resulting wine amazed all of us. In addition, it whetted my appetite still further to produce wine

19

one day from grapes that I myself had grown. The field across the brook I now knew would not do. What I needed was a sloping, sunny, dry location of about five acres where I could indulge my hobby—for of course it was always going to be a hobby. Then, with a sudden snap, the net was closed.

A certain justice of the peace, about whom another book could be written, came to me one scorching August day and asked if I'd ever heard of High Tor. It seemed that it was for sale, and at a very reasonable price. Of course I knew the rocky point on the Palisades above Haverstraw called High Tor. I even was familiar with the play of the same name by Maxwell Anderson, although at the time I had never read it through. Despite the Pulitzer Prize it received, it was, and is, a bore. But I was intrigued with the idea of walking over historic ground, seeing at first hand the little that remains of a mountain estimated to be one of the oldest above ground in the entire world; an 870-foot rock that was once higher than Mount Everest; a rock on which Henry Hudson left part of his crew to keep a bonfire going to guide him on his return down what is now the Hudson River. That was the extent of my interest. I was looking for five acres, not seventy-eight. I already had my comfortable Victorian house, so who needed the two more that this property boasted?

We walked the complete boundaries of the property in the company of the seventy-five-year-old caretaker, to whom a third of the property had been left. I had just turned thirty-eight, but old Gus had us panting in ten minutes. The air was pure, the views were incredible, and even to the eye of a novice the grape-growing potential was real and tangible. At the end of the tour I tumbled into the car with my friend and, feigning exhaustion, drove off.

Alma, of course, had not seen it, and she was indignant that I should even consider a land investment of this size. She was right, but I couldn't get it out of my system. So I hit on all sorts of delaying tactics. One, how did I really know that the land was suitable for grapes? Call the county agent, said the justice of the peace, visions of a commission dancing like sugarplums in his head—although he later said that he did not accept a commission. So I called the county agricultural agent, who to my dismay said that he had seldom seen a better grape-growing potential. Running the line out in another direction, I asked my friend why I needed two more houses, neither with running water or electricity. I was reminded that the deed went back to George III, and that the main house was built in 1790. It would have value someday, and the price was certainly reasonable. Vainly fighting against the gaff hook, I said that reasonable or not, I couldn't afford it. Make them an offer, I was told. Any offer. So I made what I considered to be an insulting offer and with the speed of light they took it. High Tor was ours.

_2_

High Tor was ours, and the question we now faced, which any
sensible person would have faced earlier, was what to do with
it. Seventy-eight acres for people in our income bracket most
certainly could not be considered in the hobby category. There
were houses to be kept up, taxes to be paid, and I was working
for a living, although it must be said that the work was not all
that time-consuming. While writing regularly for radio, I had
begun writing for the new medium, television. In addition, I
was directing a series of special dramatic programs for the
Voice of America, and this required my presence in the city
three days a week. But I am a fairly fast writer and I certainly
had more free time to spend on a new venture than the average
commuter.

In our innocence we thought it would be possible to establish
a commercial vineyard, build a winery and enter the wine business while still keeping up the three-day commute. Of course it
was possible at first while the young vines grew and before we
had any crop to contend with. But in 1955 I wrote my last
script, and was able to do that only by staying up night after

night. It was either the vineyard or writing, and by now our dedication to the vineyard was complete.

We took title to what was then called the Van Orden farm in January of 1950 and took stock of what we owned. There were two houses on the property, one a summer bungalow whose roof leaked, the other a fascinating farmhouse built around 1790, with rafters of hand-hewn cedar beams held together with wooden pegs. The house had been lengthened by an addition in about 1890—the "new wing." There was a barn in such a state of disrepair that the advice of one and all was to tear it down and save what beams we could.

Of our seventy-eight acres, some was in the township of Haverstraw, the bulk in the township of Clarkstown. (This has resulted in our having two congressmen—a fact of some importance, as will be mentioned—for the congressional district splits along these town lines.) Most of the land is rolling, but part of it was a boulder-strewn precipice rising up to the summit of High Tor. I should add that this summit had been acquired by the Palisades Interstate Park Commission from the Van Orden estate some years before we acquired the remainder. Originally nearly all of it had been farmed, but as Elmer, the last of the Van Ordens, grew older the cultivated section shrank steadily back upon the house until at his death in 1942 only about fifteen acres immediately surrounding the house showed any trace of ever having been cleared. And even on these the jungle was steadily encroaching.

A word about the Van Ordens. The Dutch influence is particularly heavy in this part of the state, and before the influx of newcomers to Rockland County the section of the telephone book beginning with "Van" was one of the largest. I have been told that as recently as 1900 the services in the Reformed Church at West Nyack were conducted in Dutch. The name Van Orden is a corruption of the Dutch words *van norden*—

from the north. And this family had apparently acquired the farm by marriage when Charity Youmans, from a family that had extensive land holdings in the area, married the man who was to become Elmer Van Orden's father sometime about the middle of the last century.

Elmer never married, and when his father died he advertised for a boy to do some part-time work. Thus it was that one August Weltie, an orphan from Germany apprenticed from an orphanage in Brooklyn to the brickworks in Haverstraw, walked over High Tor Mountain one day in 1892 to apply for the temporary position. He stayed for almost sixty years, never in all that time receiving a dollar in pay, working for bed and board alone. He was illiterate, but in the roistering politics of those days that meant nothing. Wagons came around every election day to carry Democratic voters to Haverstraw, and Gus voted many a year before it was discovered that he was not a citizen. But he remedied this defect and in the process taught himself to read and write, and when Elmer died he left the property divided evenly between Gus, a nephew and a niece. He also left Gus the right to live in the house, but nothing on which to live, which was the reason that my low offer was accepted with such alacrity. Gus was a well-known local figure, and when he died at the age of eighty-nine many prominent people were present at the funeral.

There was neither electricity nor running water when we took possession. As nothing would be possible, including pumping water, without electricity, we took care of that first. The beacon atop High Tor was supplied from a pole just outside our gate so the distance was not too great. The public utility company said it would require three poles to get to the house, only one of which would be free. After much negotiating we convinced them that we were going to build a winery, and that we would also electrify the little summer cottage that went with the place.

On the promise of three meters the company put in all three poles and ran the wires to the house; we put in the most minimal inside wiring and the first problem was solved.

The second problem—water—we couldn't tackle until the ground thawed, permitting us to dig to a depth below the frost line, which at that spot was thirty-six inches. A never failing spring, with the most delicious water I have ever tasted, had supplied the Van Ordens and their predecessors for two hundred years, via the hand-carried bucket. Happily, though, this spring was about eight feet higher than the ground outside the house, an ample drop to allow the water to run by gravity through our pipeline and into a two-hundred-gallon cistern buried near the house. From there a bargain-priced pump, bought at a fire sale, pumped the water into a pressure tank indoors. A temporary system, we thought then, but still the system in use today.

That taken care of, we turned our attention to the land. There were about fifteen acres that were reasonably clear, where the encroaching brush could be cut and plowed under. These we decided to plant a year from the upcoming spring. The county agent recommended a farmer to us, and advised that we cut our figure about in half, concentrating on the eight best acres for the first planting. As soon as the weather was warm enough he would supply a crew of semiretired farmers, itching for the chance to work in the open again, to clear the small brush by hand. Then we would plow.

I had never even sat in a tractor seat, but again with the advice of the county agent I bought an International Farmall Super "A" tractor with hydraulic lift. I also bought a moldboard plow, a three-gang vineyard plow, a heavy disk harrow and a set of cultivator teeth that attached to the hydraulic lift. And on a fine spring day I mounted my new toy, and following my farming instructor, John Mein, on his own tractor, learned to plow. He plowed a furrow, while I rode along behind with a wheel in that furrow and plowed another. By the end of the day I was ready to plow on my own.

None of this ground had been plowed for ten or more years, and the accumulated "trash" on the surface was inches thick. This rich organic overlay was turned back into the soil to decompose and feed the roots of the young vines to be planted later. The subsoil came to the top, and this we disked until it was smooth. A light dressing of fertilizer was now applied by hand, the two of us walking abreast with canvas bags slung from our shoulders, flinging out the contents with measured motions of hand and arm. Now we were ready for a cover crop.

After some discussion it was decided to use soybeans and golden millet, the soybeans for the nitrogen-fixing power of the legume family, the golden millet for its organic bulk. Again we walked through the fields with our sacks, looking like a painting from the Flemish school. The seeds were turned in by running over them with the disk in the almost fully open position, and that part of the operation was complete.

I was learning to be a farmer, but of winemaking all I knew was what I had learned from making fifty or so gallons a year from my miserable swamp-grown grapes and the mediocre California grapes mentioned earlier. As I have always believed that when you have a problem you go immediately to the top, I called Frank Schoonmaker and made an appointment.

Something that has never ceased to interest me is the dedication and the total involvement of the wine community. You can go to any winemaker in the world and say that you are a student of the vine. If this is in fact the case—and it doesn't take a true wine man long to find out—the world is yours. Ask any question and you get an honest answer. In my own experience, visitors to a winery are divided almost equally between people who have come sincerely to learn and those who want to impress on us how much they know. In almost every instance the second group knows very little and constitutes a major pain in the derrière. I recall a man who assured me that he owned one of the major wine and liquor stores in New York City, and had organized a small self-glorifying wine-testing society. He came with his wife, who on seeing that much of our equipment came from Germany said to her husband, "Why so much German machinery? They don't make any good wines in Germany." Her husband's admonishing glance was wasted on her, but at that moment I had the picture. So later, when I gave them a sample of a certain vintage with the statement "All the experts who have tried it say it's our best so far," I was not surprised to hear them say with the unanimity of a Greek chorus, "We don't agree with the experts." I could not resist saying, "How unfortunate for you."

But Frank Schoonmaker is something else again. I doubt if anyone knows the logistics of the American wine business better, and at the beginning of that first interview he behaved toward me as I later behaved toward visitors at High Tor Vineyards. Was I or was I not the real thing? Once he was convinced that I was, I could not have been given more or better advice. The plateaus of operation, the amount of wine that a one-man operation could produce and at what point a profit could be expected were all carefully explained. I am afraid that had I heard this before I bought High Tor I might never have made the purchase. But since I had, this man felt an obligation to see that I made the best of it. He thought that I should visit the Finger Lakes wineries and get the story from their side. But he was adamant that I go to Maryland and visit Phillip Wagner, the proprietor of Boordy Vineyard, and the man who brought the Franco-American hybrids to this country. By now, of course, I knew quite a bit about the hybrids, but I had never tasted any wine made from them. Naturally I took Mr. Schoonmaker's advice.

Meanwhile, the soybeans and the golden millet grew like mad beasts in the potential vineyards and by midsummer the millet was a good five feet tall. Never having seen a copperhead, and not really believing there were any in the area, without a qualm we permitted our eight-year-old daughter to run through plants that were over a foot taller than she was. We would see the tall grain waving and know that she was in there somewhere. Every time I kill a copperhead today a cold feeling comes over me when I consider the possibilities.

God, however, was good, and in midsummer we all took a trip to the Finger Lakes to visit the Widmer Winery at Naples, New York. It was a Widmer product that first turned me on to New York wines, and it was naturally the winery I wanted to see the most. The Widmer brothers, in the tradition of all true wine men, could not have been kinder. Will Widmer showed us through the winery itself, and Frank Widmer devoted the rest of the day to showing us around the vineyards. I sincerely believe that the Widmer brothers made the best wine that it was possible to make out of the grapes then available to them. In fact, Louis Martini said to me some years later that he considered Will Widmer to be the best white-wine maker in America. His only trouble was that he didn't have the proper grape to work with.

A week or so later we made an appointment to visit Boordy Vineyard in Maryland to see the hybrids at first hand. Again we got the cursory treatment until our winemaking dedication was established and then the carpet unrolled. We saw the grapes growing, small compact vines growing without the bulky pruning systems required by the old-fashioned varieties, and simply loaded with fruit. Then we went back to the winery and tried the wine. Not the greatest wine in the world (to be candid I must add that I do not believe anything grown in this country including our own is in that class), it still so much more nearly resembled wine as we knew it than anything we had tasted in

28

New York and all but a tiny number in California that the choice as to what we would plant was on the moment resolved. We wound up ordering 3,500 vines to fill the land we would have ready the following spring, and we left the choice to Phillip and Jocelyn Wagner. They assured us that we must expect some failures, for their knowledge of how the hybrid would do in New York was limited to a few experimental plantings around the Finger Lakes. We would be the first commercial winery in New York to produce its wine entirely from the Franco-American hybrids.

The varieties the Wagners chose were purposely designed not to ripen all at the same time. This was to keep us from being inundated with more grapes than we could handle at any given time, and to allow the grapes to be fermented in a certain vat and moved on to another container, while the first vat would then be free to handle the next-ripening variety.

Hybrid grapes do not, or did not until recently, have glamorous names. Rather they are named for the hybridizer who developed them and the number of the particular cross that produced them. Thus Seibel 13053 means that on the thirteen thousand and fifty-third cross-pollination, Mr. Seibel came up with something he considered good enough to assign a number to. Baco #1 means that Mr. Baco was unusually lucky.

Now, however, a group of New York winegrowers has been assigning fancy names to these grape varieties—French names. Thus Seibel 5279 becomes "Aurore," Baco #1 is "Baco Noir," Seyve-Villard 5-276 becomes "Seyval Blanc," Seibel 10878 "Chelois," and on and on, ad nauseam and ad ludicrum, if such a phrase exists. If it doesn't it should. Why any self-respecting American winegrower would take a grape with the blood of American vines flowing in its veins, produced to grow and prosper in American soil and American climate, and then tack a hokey French name on it surpasseth my understanding. I will have much to say in a later section about genuflection before the "imported" syndrome, and this is all part of it. I stick with the names those brilliant hybridizers proudly gave them.

The varieties we were to plant turned out to be Seibel 5279, a very early-season white; Seibel 13047, a similar white that ripens about a week later; Seyve-Villard 5-276, a midseason white; and Seibel 4986, a late white.

The reds included Seibel 13053, an early and lightly colored variety; Baco #1, a midseason deeper grape; and Seibel 7053, a late and quite deeply colored variety.

Of these, S. 13047 was a total failure, and after coddling it for nine years we pulled it up. In later years "Foch," a very popular variety, and Ravat 244 also failed. The rest took a while to adapt, but now grow extremely well, as have later additions of Landot 262 and Seibel 8357.

Then it was time to turn the lush green growth of the summer once more into the soil, and with the assistance of my farmer friend we did this and sowed a generous planting of winter rye. There was nothing to do in the vineyards now but await the arrival of the young vines the following spring. So we turned our attention to the main house. The water supply system had been taken care of, and an attached lean-to woodshed was converted into a bathroom by installing a secondhand basin, toilet and flimsy tin stall shower. In this way I learned one of the basic skills that one needs for the wine business—plumbing. After many a leaky joint and many a curse I became reasonably adept at what is known as "sweating" a joint and filled the lower part of the house with open copper piping which, at a later date, we had to go to the expense of boxing in. It never occurred to either of us that we would ever use the house for anything but rough summer camping. Had anyone ever suggested that in six years it would become our main residence, or that we would spend over $35,000 on it, we would have sent him straight to the nearest available psychiatrist. But that's exactly what happened.

Although I have now become a competent electrician, I wisely brought in a professional to wire the rest of the house. We told him not to bother with appearances, and the hand-hewn oak beams were crisscrossed with BX cable, all of which was later relocated. And because we didn't want to go to the expense of installing a regular heating system in a house we would never use in the winter, we had the electrician simply put a few electric heaters in the wall. Most of these we had to remove later, and the rest still squat on the wall, the vestigial remains of our unwise penny-pinching.

The winter passed quickly and one day in March we got a notice from Railway Express that several large bundles had arrived from Maryland. The grapevines. Hastily summoning my farmer friend, I took my new tractor out of winter storage and with much slipping and sliding in the still wet ground we turned the winter rye under. My friend assembled the same geriatric group who had helped to clear the land, but before they put in an appearance Alma and I marked off a field and planted the first hundred vines. It was a gesture, but it was more than that. Every one of these old men was a retired farmer, and every one knew how everything connected with the soil was done. No possibility of change existed for any one of them. By showing them what it was supposed to look like we nipped off the endless debates that certainly would otherwise have followed. Not that mistakes didn't still crop up, like planting seventy-five of one variety right across the center of a field that was to hold six hundred of another variety. They're still there, and they ripen a month later than the rest of the field. Another thing I remember from that time is the advice given me by one of the oldest and most wizened of the workers. I was sitting on a large rock one cold morning in mid-March, trimming and separating the vines, when he approached, doffed his fur cap and said, "I wouldn't do that, boss." "Do what?" I said. "Sit on a cold rock. Surest way to get piles." The funny thing is that up until then I had been troubled with the little devils, but from the moment I sat on that cold rock I never had another. So much for home remedies.

The grapes all planted, we worked sporadically on making the house "livable"—i.e., bringing any item of furniture we didn't want up from our house in West Nyack. The random-width soft pine flooring had had linoleum nailed over it, and I spent some days with a nail puller to get it ready for sanding. I pulled what I could and drove the rest out of sight. But when I rented a floor sander and started to remove the accumulation of 160 years, a triumphantly fugitive nail would be encountered, and when that happened the sandpaper belt shredded in seconds. But I did finally complete the job and together we finished the surface, and when we saw the result it began to dawn on us that we might just perhaps have been a trifle cavalier in our evaluation of the old house. So on to the beams, painted in alternate layers of calcimine and oil paint, which made any paint remover totally ineffective. The outermost layer was battleship gray deck enamel, a favorite color of the previous owner. A large, unprepossessing chest of this same color lay on the trash heap after old Gus had auctioned off the furniture a year earlier, and when I brought it back in the house strictly for its utilitarian value I was told by a friend in the antique business that it was an old jelly cabinet, and actually quite valuable. I stripped off the deck enamel, sanded it down, and today it is one of our prized possessions. So we confidently started on the battleship gray of the beams, but after getting through that coat—approximately the ninth—we hit white calcimine, bilious green oil paint, then more calcimine, then brown deck enamel, then calcimine, and on and on. Every rainy day we scraped with paint scrapers, and when we got to bare wood we stopped. As a result faint tinges of white, green, brown and other assorted colors show through the clear finish, but this pleases us, for it reminds us of our triumph over the accumulated bad tastes of the centuries. Actually not so much bad taste as ill-considered whims, for though both Elmer and Gus were bachelors, certain females of the species did share the premises with them from time to time, and one can imagine that each succeeding layer represented a bow to the newest arrival.

I cultivated the vines frequently during that first year, with the wheels of the tractor set in the narrowest position so that I could crisscross the fields through the nine-foot-wide rows with six-foot spaces between the vines. At the last cultivation the vines had grown enough so that Alma walked ahead of me, holding back the more rampantly growing shoots from the cultivator teeth. Another sowing of winter rye, and we were bedded down for the season.

It was time now to consider the winery. We again drove down to see the Phillip Wagners in Maryland, seeing what they had done, profiting by their mistakes. Let me say that they made few mistakes. But Phil Wagner did say that he wished his roof were a few inches taller, and set nine feet as the absolute minimum height. Today I would say ten. We were again fortified by the quality of the wines we tasted, as well as by some practical advice on zoning. Boordy Vineyard operates in a highly restricted residential zone, as do we. In fact, before we bought the property we had obtained an opinion by the New York State attorney general that a winery producing most of its own grapes came under the same heading as a cider mill—an agricultural processing house. So if farming was permitted under the zoning of our area, and it was, then a winery could be built to process the grapes we grew. I had planned to construct a relatively short building, two stories high, to follow the classic flow pattern of crushing and fermenting the grapes on the upper floor, then sending them by gravity down to the cool lower floor for storing and aging. But I was told that adding horizontally to a building that might by a later ordinance become a noncon-forming use was much more difficult than adding to it vertically, and I revised my plans to a long single-story building designed to accommodate a second floor at some later time. That second floor is still waiting.

Back at the vineyards I contacted my friend the wily justice of the peace, who pointed out that the current zoning inspector was a licensed architect. I thought that ploy looked a little bald, but my friend suggested that I talk to the man in question. In this case, at least, he turned out to be right, for not only was he a good architect, but a graduate of one of the leading Scottish universities. I believe he was also a fellow of the Royal Architectural Society. How he wound up as zoning inspector in the town of Clarkstown still defeats me.

So a winery was designed, which came with a built-in building permit, and the bids were let out. I learned another lesson. If three or four reputable builders are bunched together at the bottom, take the best of them. If they are bunched in the middle and Mr. Nobody puts in a much cheaper bid, forget him. He probably can't fulfill the contract. If somebody is so much higher than the rest as to be out of sight, it means he doesn't want the contract and is only bidding to establish that he is a quality builder. This is exactly what happened. One bid was three thousand dollars below the nearest above him. Three were bunched within a thousand dollars in the middle, and the last was almost five thousand dollars above anybody.

My architect studied the bids and suggested that I accept the highest of the three bunched in the middle. "They're all good," he said, "but with only a thousand separating them he'll give you the best value." And with a few minor reservations this is the way it turned out.

So the work began, and immediately the by now expected problems began. A spring was struck, and water literally gushed a foot up into the air. A pipe was laid and the water was led off to an area where it would do some good. Then the thing I feared most, bedrock. High Tor's "mountain" is a nub of rock, worn down over the millennia by wind and water from God knows what majestic heights to 870 feet above sea level. The topsoil is minimal, and only in pockets does it have any depth. Without probing it is hard to know where the pockets really exist. We probed before starting construction, but only by digging is it possible to tell a ledge of solid rock eight feet beneath the surface from a boulder that can be moved. Well, we hit that ledge of solid rock, a ledge that is part of eternity, a ledge you could drill until you hit the fiery center of the earth.

There are many myths and many facts surrounding High Tor. One fact, according to many geologists, is that it is one of the oldest points of land above the surface of today's oceans. It is certain that the summit is seamed and lined with deep furrows and scratches made by the many recurring glaciers that have ground over its gradually dwindling height. Another fact is that a native cactus grows on its steep slopes, almost the only wild cactus growing east of the Mississippi. That High Tor was considered sacred to the Indians was well known to the early Dutch settlers. Many Indian artifacts have been found in the narrow caves that dot the sheer cliffs facing the Hudson. One of the most perfect arrowheads I have ever seen was found by a boy I was paying to hoe the grapes but who spent most of his time looking for Indian relics. I am glad that before I fired him he at least found one.

The myths are something else. The late Danton Walker was fascinated by ghostly legends, and he told me two concerning High Tor. One was that the mountain was said to be the equivalent of Pandora's Box, the evils of the world lying uneasily just beneath the surface. If one dug deeply enough they would come surging out and the world would be destroyed. Another legend held that the three Wise Men came here; why or how is never said. The legend of three holy men wandering in search of a prophet is common to many peoples and many religions, and this is probably an Indian variant. Old Gus told me it was popularly believed that the mountain was really a vast hollow shell, completely filled with water. This water made direct contact with the Hudson, and when an occasional eel or crawfish appeared in the brook it was supposed to have come via this underground passage. The spring that supplies our house has never been known to fail, always cold in the hottest weather, never freezing in the coldest. It is said that George Washington watered his horse there.

Naturally with such a background the tales of ghosts are legion. We have heard heavy boots tramping restlessly through the attic, though it has never disturbed us. I can't say as much for one of the plumbers who helped with the first water system. He was a huge man, and the tiny but literate boss on the job privately referred to him as "Lenny," after the character in *Of Mice and Men*. This enormous man refused to work alone in the house, and finally his boss asked in exasperation, "Why the hell are you afraid of ghosts?"

The big man stared at him somberly and said, "Them things bite."

One final true story concerning a local ghost. There was a persistent legend that a beautiful girl had died of a broken heart in a house near the foot of our hill. She haunted this house for years, and many a witness has sworn to looking up suddenly and seeing her standing at the head of the stairs. Danton Walker asked old Elmer Van Orden if he had ever seen her, and Elmer replied, "Seen her? Hell, I used to go with her."

Maxwell Anderson's Pulitzer Prize-winning play *High Tor* was based on this same Elmer Van Orden's running battle with the New York Trap Rock Corporation, which wanted to buy High Tor from him and blast it down for paving stones. Elmer never sold, but in the play that character, finally realizing that the destruction is inevitable, gives up and sells. Elmer never forgave Anderson for that. Who knows whether Elmer, with his Dutch background, believed in the Pandora's Box legend? Perhaps he was afraid to go down to posterity as the man who let unrestricted fatality loose on the world. I thought of it myself when I came to the ledge under the winery, and refrained from blasting. Also, it was frightfully expensive.

So we had to alter the plans. The back room, the one with the deficient depth, would be eight feet six inches under the ground. The rest, the part for the big casks and stacks of barrels, would be the nine feet the master called for. I still wish I had blasted and gone for ten.

Winter arrived and found us with the walls of the eighty-by-forty-foot building up, the concrete floors poured, the roof beams up, but no roof. And when it became apparent that the snow, the sleet and the ice were not transient but were socked in for the season, all work stopped. We were in no hurry, being a year and a half away from our first commercial production. Draining the water pipes in the house and turning off our new electricity, we went back to the West Nyack house, the house we were sure we would live in for the rest of our lives. The winter settled in, the steep gravel road became impassable and the new vineyards slept. All was well.

It now seemed reasonable to learn something about winemaking, and so once more I went to Frank Schoonmaker to get a list of people I should see on a visit to Europe planned for the upcoming summer. I didn't want to go to Château Lafite Rothschild, or Romanée-Conti, or even such great German wineries as Schloss Johannisberg and Schloss Vollrads. I wanted to see the small makers of good wine, and I knew that as a buyer of vinous exotica Mr. Schoonmaker would know who these people were. Again he was most generous of his time and compiled a rather lengthy list. I was quite let down when another well-known man in the wine business, a man who previously had been most helpful, declined to give me names, saying that he would rather not take advantage of his European friends by sending a stranger into their homes. As it turned out I didn't need him.

As soon as our daughter—by now ten—was out of school for the summer we sailed on the *Queen Elizabeth* for Southampton and London, to pick up a car I had ordered in New York. Here, for the first time, I encountered the classic run-around the British can give you if they feel like putting down the Yankees. I also found out how helpful they can be if they have forgotten the empire and want to cooperate. And it was someone in the latter category, a man with the unlikely name of Muckett, who untangled the red tape, chided the obfuscators, cleared our papers and put us in our spanking new Rover with only minutes to spare, on the road that led to the *Golden Arrow,* the express boat that carried us and our car to Calais.

None of us had made a Channel crossing before, and who hasn't heard of the pitching and rolling horrors when the sea is acting up, as it frequently is? So shortly before arriving at Dover we all swallowed a generous supply of Dramamine to be on the safe side.

I have seldom if ever seen a calmer sea. You could look over the side and see your reflection in the water, and over this glassy millpond we skimmed to Calais. But the Dramamine had done its deadly work, and shortly after disembarking and heading south on the beautiful French roads, none of us could keep our eyes open. At a quarter to five we came to a small inn, and I stumbled through the door and asked if they could feed us and put us up for the night. It took them a minute or two to understand what I was talking about, for while some people deprecate their "high school" French, I never studied French in any school, having picked it up more or less through the skin. The result is that I speak French quite volubly, but fantastically ungrammatically. Finally I did make myself understood and simply overrode their objections as to the early hour. We were served a quick and, considering the circumstances, excellent meal, and shortly after six we were all in bed, sleeping the clock around.

The scars of World War II were still much in evidence in 1952, and we hurried through the Normandy countryside as quickly as we could, and in France that is very quickly indeed. A few days in Paris to eat and to drink and to soak up that fabulous city, and then off to our first wine stop, the Loire. We had one of the names Frank Schoonmaker had given us, a family who had a *cave* in Vouvray. I should point out that in Vouvray a *cave* is quite literally a cave, sometimes ninety feet deep under the limestone cliffs. We found the proprietor in, and he couldn't have been more friendly and cooperative. We looked at the vineyards, looked at the winery, tasted the wine. Everyone was astonished that we considered our ten-year-old daughter too young to taste it. Six was the age that delightful practice was started in France. To show our appreciation we bought a couple of bottles of wine, not knowing that our host was doing us a favor. He was too polite to refuse our request, but if he had been caught selling untax-paid wine he could have been in serious trouble. In France the tax is collected from the retailer, whereas in America it is paid by the winery before it ever goes on the market.

We spent the night in Tours at a hotel boasting a two-star restaurant, and as in most two-star restaurants with ambitions for that third star, the night was alive with flames as everything was incinerated at the table. Then on to Bordeaux and our first encounter with the Médoc peninsula. Here we found the first variation on a theme, a variation we were to encounter again and again. The man recommended by Mr. Schoonmaker—by now we were used to calling him Monsieur Shoon-mah-*caire*—had made a most fortunate sale, we were told by his wife. And he had that morning departed for the city of Bordeaux with a wagonload of wine, and would probably not be back for at least a day. There was a one-star restaurant—naturally I am referring to the *Guide Michelin* ratings—nearby which had a few rooms to rent. We checked in and had a simple but excellent meal, and during the course of it I found out something of the way the Michelin system works. I said to the proprietor's wife that if they continued to serve the quality meal we had received they would soon have two stars. She threw her hands to her face.

"Disaster," she said.

We were puzzled. "Why disaster?"

"Because if we got two stars we would have to buy all new china, new glasses, new linen, new kitchenware. Believe me, monsieur, two stars would put us out of business."

Perhaps the most fascinating thing about this inn was the plumbing. Although it had inside toilets, it was nothing but an enormous outhouse. There were three floors to the building, and everything dropped into the same pit. It gave one a certain feeling of exaltation to sit on the third floor and think of the final product's soaring thirty-foot flight. Made you feel good for an entire day.

On hearing that we had come to visit wineries, and that the man we had come to see was away, our host at the inn sent me to his cousin who had a winery around the corner that was in the same category as the one we had missed. We had a most pleasant and instructive time there, and then the owner insisted on taking us himself to Château d'Yquem. My driving almost gave him a nervous breakdown, for the French are great horn tooters and I was raised to believe that the horn is the weapon of last resort. A good driver drives with his eyes, a poor one with his ears. I still feel this way.

At the château I was reminded of one of our daughter's more laudable traits: intense family loyalty. When she was five I was writing, among other bits of nonsense, the Dick Tracy radio show. Averil had a cocker spaniel named Ginger, and I put such a dog into one of the stories. Naturally this dog had to get into trouble. Everyone and everything *always* had to get into trouble. But when I realized that Averil believed it was all happening, I took her to a broadcast to convince her that it wasn't really her Ginger on the railroad trestle with the train approaching. She watched the stolid, portly man who was the chief animal impersonator of his day whimper and sniffle and bark, but somehow her lively imagination would not let her blot out the real Ginger. And at that moment we were told that one of the sponsors was coming to the control room. I took Averil aside and told her how important it was to Daddy for him to like the show. Please don't cry. So the show went on, and the episode ended with the locomotive rumbling over the spot where Ginger was supposed to be cowering. I knew Averil was petrified, even as she watched the whimpering gray-haired gentleman who portrayed Ginger, and was certainly in no immediate danger of his life. But she had an artificial smile the size of all outdoors plastered on her face, a smile that any father would know was totally phony. And when the program was over, sure enough the sponsor said, "And how did you like the show, little girl?"

Stretching the smile to the breaking point, she said, "I liked it fine."

At Château d'Yquem the same thing happened. Although to me the wine is too sweet for all but the most limited use, it is nevertheless one of the most magnificent wines in the world. And when they offered it to our daughter we felt she should try some. God knows it was too expensive for *me* to be passing around. Also, we thought that the sweetness might make it more palatable to a child. But we counted without all those teetotaling ancestors in both our families, and it was immediately clear to Alma and me that she simply loathed it. The plastic smile once more spread itself on her face, however, as once more she spoke the magic words "I liked it fine."

Then on to Spain. Years before I had spent several weeks in that marvelous country, and I was anxious to visit it again.

When Alma and I made a bicycle tour of Europe in 1937 the Spanish Civil War was still raging, and a visit was out of the question. So now I was to show it to my wife and daughter for the first time.

Spanish I have studied, and ungrammatical I am not. But I don't speak it as fluently as French, because I picked up the latter as a child learns a language, and the former as an adult does. I can conjugate verbs, including the subjunctive, all afternoon. But the mystical thing that makes conversation possible is missing, and all my comments must be thought out carefully in advance. I was, however, able to help out four young Danes at the border who spoke just about every language under the sun except Spanish, and who were mystified that none of the border guards spoke anything but Spanish. Carefully putting this in the form of a question, I asked why it was so. With a look of astonishment one of them replied, "But this is Spain, señor. Why should we speak anything else?" They had me there.

We drove through San Sebastián, and on to the town of Zarauz. And if you don't think they lisp in this part of the country, try asking the directions to Zaragoza. If you don't say "Tharagotha," forget it. They won't know what you're talking about. In Tharauth we found one hotel open, El Gran Hotel. It was indeed grand, a long palm-lined drive leading to a most imposing structure facing the Bay of Biscay. It was the only hotel open because this was the summer vacation area of Spain, and we were a bit early. I have never ceased to be amazed that each country in Europe is a world unto itself. Entering France in Normandy we were in the north, where apples are grown. Driving south we came into ever more tropical vegetation and architecture until at the Spanish border it was all red-tiled roofs and palms and oranges. Crossing the border into the north of Spain, we were back to apples and pears again, even though the sub-tropical part of France was only ten miles to the north. And it

42

was to this relatively cool part of Spain that wealthy families came to escape the even hotter summers of the south.

But El Gran Hotel looked somewhat too grand for our already overstrained budget and we drove past in the direction of Santander. We never reached this city for one simple reason. It was Sunday, and everyone was out wheeling the baby, and everyone *has* a baby. At that time not much in the way of durable goods was made in Spain. But I have never seen better-built baby buggies. They have to be, for they are in use daily. I doubt if they ever cool off between babies. And these buggies clogged the coast road, until it became obvious that we would never reach the next town before the sudden night fell. So we turned around, and threading our careful way through the buggies we returned to Zarauz.

We pulled up across the street from the imposing hotel, all of us tired from our drive, and finally I said, "I don't care what it costs, we all need a good night's sleep. One night here, and then we'll find a cheap place."

The lord had spoken, and I went in to negotiate. The young woman at the counter listened to my Spanish for a minute or so and then asked in impeccable English what we would need. God, I thought, there goes the price through the ceiling. She showed me a two-room suite, with a large bathroom containing one of the biggest tubs I have ever seen and a balcony overlooking the beach and the Bay of Biscay, and she quoted the price for the three of us with three meals a day. I was new to the peseta, but it looked like $7.50 a day.

"Apiece?" I said.

"No, señor. All three."

I went back to the car in a daze, got out a piece of paper and figured the peseta price every way I knew how. It still turned out to be $7.50 a day. So we took it and spent almost two weeks there putting our battered budget back in shape.

We also visited the winery of the Marqués de Murrieta, in the Rioja district, one of the best wineries in the best table wine district of Spain. I don't know what the telephone situation in Spain is today, but at that time there were no long-line cables between any but the major cities, and to make the appointment a *conferencia* was arranged. The operator in Zarauz called the operator in the next town and asked the best route to Logroño. The second operator would then contact another one somewhere to the south, and this would continue until five operators were holding a conference, the last one being in the town of Logroño. Then the English-speaking lady in the hotel office got on and started to tell the office manager of the winery that an American was— At which point she would say loudly and indignantly, *"Oiga!"*—"Listen." But there was no one to listen, as one or another of the five operators would inadvertently have pulled the wrong plug. Finally, on about the tenth try she did get it across that an American winemaker would be coming to visit the next morning. This fact was barely acknowledged when the line went dead altogether.

After an early start, we got to the winery at about eleven and were met by *el escribiente,* the office manager, and *el técnico,* the winemaker. Much of what was true of a later visit to Undurraga Winery in Chile was true of this justly famous winery, for machinery was almost nonexistent. They were bottling red wine when we got there, and it was being pumped from three floors below to a wooden tub on a platform, whence it flowed by gravity into the bottle filler. A man squatted beside this tub constantly filling and emptying a clear glass with the wine and holding it briefly in front of a light. At the first hint of sediment he called down the air chute and the pump was turned off, the line was drained and the hose shifted to the next barrel. After about every half-dozen or so glasses, one would be passed on to the workers, men and women, so that the whole operation had become happy and boisterous.

The red wine was exceedingly good, but I found the white barely drinkable, owing to the fact that the Spaniards like their white wine aged to the point of no return. After all, they are the people who invented sherry, an intentionally oxidized wine. Here, when one of our white wines oxidizes and turns dark in color and assumes a sherrylike flavor—spoils, in other words— we say that it has "madeirized"—that it has taken on the taste of madeira. Why madeira and not sherry, I don't know, but it's the same thing. Fine in sherry, murder in table wine. But Spaniards like this flavor in their quality white wines, and when we were there in 1952, they were bottling a 1937 white—*fifteen* years in the wood. No one but a Spaniard could have drunk it.

I still had a bottle of Vouvray we had bought at the winery two weeks earlier, and I opened it and gave some to *el técnico,* telling him that it was only six months old. He sniffed it cautiously, took the professional winemaker's gurgling sip, swished it around in his mouth and spit it out.

"Not bad," he said. "Not bad for six months."

An interesting sidelight to this is that when Spain began to push her wines on the world market, the officials were puzzled as to why no other country bought any of their white. It took them quite a while to realize that they alone liked their wines to taste that way. And as America was the big market they were after, they finally brought in a young winemaker from Fresno, California, to show them how to make white wines that were more to the taste of the rest of the world.

The trip back to Zarauz was entirely fascinating. The country surrounding the grape-growing district is among the most barren in the world, and coming from California I know what barren means. Rocks and red dust, with here and there a small cultivated patch. Frequently the plowing was done by the man of the family pulling the plow by a rope, while his wife guided. And just as frequently the motive power was reversed. In the

45

Spain of 20 years ago, to be mechanized meant to own a mule.

A few miles out of Logroño we came to a small river, with vegetation extending perhaps twenty feet on either side. Parking under a lone tree, we ate the excellent lunch the Gran Hotel Zarauz had put up for us, and then decided to stay in the shade until it got cooler. Thus it was that just at dusk we came through a rocky pass and stopped to admire the view below. As we did we heard the sound of a primitive flute playing melancholy Moorish tunes, tunes still part of the lives of the Spanish people more than five hundred years after the Moors have gone. The flute was being played by a solitary shepherd boy following a small band of sheep, and we watched and listened until both the sight and the sound were gone.

Leaving Zarauz, we spent a night in Zaragoza, and then on to Barcelona. We drove down the beautiful Rambla de Cataluña and pulled up in front of the same hotel where I had stayed on my maiden trip in 1929. Unfortunately, while trying to book rooms I made a mistake in arithmetic and said to the clerk that I had stayed there sixteen years earlier, instead of twenty-three. Sixteen years earlier would have been right in the midst of the Spanish Civil War and Barcelona was the last place to surrender to the forces of Generalissimo Franco. The clerk gave me a stony look and said there were no rooms available. We had to go to the hotel next door, where I had the sense to keep my mouth shut.

Driving up the Rhone, once more in our relentless pursuit of the gospel according to Saint Bacchus, we stopped to visit a Mlle. Chierpe, a perfectly charming maiden lady whose Hermitage wines regularly won prizes at various expositions, and who cheerily told us that at least three times as much wine was marketed as "Hermitage" than could possibly be grown in the district. Hers was a tiny winery, about to become more tiny. Why? we asked. It seemed that the French equivalent of a thruway or freeway was scheduled to pass through her property,

46

and that the rapid movement of automobiles was much more important than an acre or so of priceless vineyard land. We sighed, as the New York State Thruway was even then in the process of ruining Rockland County.

But the wonderful memory I have of this indomitable woman concerns a certain phase of the vinification of red wines. At the time of the primary fermentation it used to be the practice in France for naked men to jump into the vats up to their armpits to break up the quickly forming crust, which if left alone would surely ruin the wine. This practice was abolished some years ago, not for sanitary reasons but because so many men were overcome by the fumes and drowned in the new wine. So as she was showing us around the winery and explaining her procedures we came to this point in the process.

"What happens here?" I asked.

"The men jump in the vats," she said.

"But isn't that illegal?"

With perfect aplomb she placed her hands an inch or so lower than her crotch and said, "They only jump in up to here, monsieur."

A Swiss guest at El Gran Hotel, on hearing that we were wine people, had touted me onto a winery named Testuz Brothers. I believe that's the spelling. In addition to their making among the best of the Swiss wines, the thing that really grabbed me was the fact that the family was said to speak perfect English. It was located on the north shore of the Lake of Geneva near the town of Montreux, so after leaving the Rhone Valley we arrived at the winery just in time to see the entire family driving off to a funeral. We had made the mistake of arriving unannounced, and I cannot use strong enough language to say how big a mistake this is. Again and again, just when I was up to my hips in some emergency at High Tor, a happy family would drive up and ask to "look around." If you let them they will be eternally underfoot, and if you don't feelings

47

are hurt and you may lose a customer. I finally trained the owner of the gas station at the foot of our hill not to point out our unmarked road unless the person inquiring said he had an appointment.

Anyway, the entire English-speaking contingent was in the car, and would not be back that day. An extremely tall red-haired Swiss said in guttural Swiss-French that he would be happy to show us around. I could barely understand a word he said, and God knows he didn't have much of a clue as to what I was saying, but there it was. As I lurched into my lumbering French Alma began to giggle, and then to guffaw. She was in an uptight condition anyway, for she suffers badly from vertigo and we had made two Alpine passes that morning. I was almost afraid that she was going to dissolve into hysteria, but she pulled herself together and the tour went on. I didn't get much out of it, but one phrase I do remember. The section around Montreux prides itself on producing the best Swiss wines, and I was incautious enough to ask what they thought of Neuchâtel. My guide pulled himself up to all his imposing six feet six and said, "Here we use Neuchâtel to scour out the vats."

We stopped briefly in Zurich to buy a small crusher-stemmer, a machine that removes the stems and crushes grapes at the same time. Nothing produced in America would be small enough for us, and I had seen one like this at Phillip Wagner's Boordy Vineyard. Then two nights in Germany's Black Forest at a charming hotel at Titisee, and on to our next to last winery.

This was in Alsace, where we had a letter introducing us to a young man named Jean Paul Blank. Luck was with us, for not only was he home but he spoke excellent English. He was busy—wine people are always busy—but he took the time to show us around. Every inch of his property had been fought over, and it was amazing how little evidence of this remained. He told us that the American tanks and artillery had been in his vineyards, and the Germans defended themselves inside his

48

winery, firing antitank guns through his windows at the American tanks maneuvering through the carefully cultivated grapes. When the Germans were finally driven out one trellis wire was still intact of all the thousands that had been there a few days earlier.

Only Burgundy remained—we were not going to Champagne this trip—and again we were lucky, for we found Henri Gouge at his winery in Nuits-St. Georges with a little time to spare for us. He is a man of strong opinions, said to be the father of the *Appellation Contrôlée* system that keeps the labels of French wine more or less honest, and although he had the customary contempt all Frenchmen whose livelihood depends on the classic grape varieties feel for the Franco-American hybrids (*"Les hybrides ne sont pas nobles"*), he was extremely instructive and informative. He made the ultimate sacrifice of digging into a secret cache and opening one of his last few bottles of the 1945 vintage. He conceded that it was not really ready to be drunk, but then none of it would last that long, and he wanted to show an earnest young student of the vine what a truly noble wine tasted like while there was still some on hand. I will never forget an answer of monumental simplicity he gave to a question I asked. Red wine is fermented together with the skins and the seeds in open tanks until all the color and character have been absorbed by the semiliquid that will go into the press. Much scientific argument goes on as to just how long this period should be. Should the new wine be "left on the skins" until this primary fermentation is totally finished, or should it be pressed off while some fermentation is still in progress? So I asked M. Gouge how long he let his wine remain in the skins. He looked at me oddly. "Until it is ready to be taken off," he replied. Stupid of me not to have known. This was not meant as a put-down. It is a thing you know or you don't know, and suddenly there comes a time when you know it.

Back in Paris we encountered the most unbearable hot spell I have ever run across in any city. I thought New York was unbeatable in this department, but Paris backed it off the map. We packed a picnic lunch and drove out to the forest of Fontainebleau, and it was even hotter there. The spongy moss that grows everywhere in this parklike "forest" steamed, the birds drooped, the sandwiches wilted in our hands. Without a pang we boarded the boat train the next day for Cherbourg and the *Queen Mary*.

The winery was by now finished. It was wired but had no plumbing, as I was determined to do this work myself. The only drawback was that I had no water supply other than the small spring which fed our house, but since we were to make no commercial wine for at least a year there was time to take care of that matter. Again I called the county agent and asked about building a reservoir. With his accustomed speed he sent a state engineer, who explained that as we did not live in a conservation district the state could not help to finance the project. They would, however, design it, lay out the grades and advise the contractor. We agreed to this and the next week he showed up, checked the topography, did some sightings with a transit and announced that the perfect site for a reservoir was about two hundred feet above the house in a swampy area which at one time was used to grow commercial cranberries. Not only did a small stream wander through it but it was alive with springs. So the design was drawn, the levels established and the whole thing let out to bid. It may seem unreal in light of today's prices that the bid we accepted for building a reservoir almost one-third of an acre in area and seven feet deep was $1,400. But the job was done, and, under the supervision of the state engineer, excellently. Vincent Kreuz, one of the German farmers who had helped plant the vines, was by now working for me steadily several hours a day, while taking care of his own farm in the time remaining. He dug by hand a four-foot-deep trench from the reservoir to the winery, five hundred feet. In this trench we laid a one-inch copper line which I later hooked up to an ancient white enamel sink. This was naturally supposed to be temporary, but like so much else it lingered on. Over the years my wife repeatedly threatened to leave me if I didn't replace it, but neither eventuality occurred.

3

We now had a completed winery, with electric lights, a solid gravity flow of water and a bottled gas heating system. The year was 1952 and the first microscopic supply of grapes was ripening. We invited fifteen or twenty of our friends to harvest this tiny supply, about fifteen bushel baskets, and put it through our spanking new crusher-stemmer from Switzerland and our ancient electric basket press that we had bought secondhand from Cribari's New York operation. About one barrel of white and perhaps fifteen gallons of red resulted, and with much ceremony we carried it to the back room, the only room with a heater. No mother hen has ever clucked over a brood of chicks with more concern than we did with this small precommercial vintage, and the resulting quality of the wine exceeded our wildest expectations. When the time came to return once more to our "real" house in West Nyack, we left our first High Tor vintage to mature gracefully in the controlled fifty-five-degree temperature of what was later to become the bottle room.

Now we had to get down to business. How do you bond a winery? How do you get a New York State winery license? What can you do, what can't you do? I wish I knew today. I doubt if there is a man alive who can accurately answer all these questions. But we wrote to both the federal and state agencies and were instantly bombarded with the maddest array of rules, regulations, yes-you-cans, no-you-can'ts, and don't-try-to-get-away-with-thises that either of us had ever seen. But we put it down to our lack of legal training and hired a lawyer friend whose office was in the immediate area of the confusing agencies. Imagine our surprise when he called somewhat later to say that he also could not make head or tail of the conflicting rules. But a start had to be made, and the federal side of the deal had to be approved before we could think of moving to get a state license. At this point the three of us sat down and tried to put everything together in logical sequence. First the application, then the bond, then the diagram and plan of the premises to be bonded, then the inspection. Put in that light it sounded rather simple. Nothing could be *that* insane.

Well, it *was* that insane. The mind of man has never been put to more perverted use than in drawing up the bonding procedures. Never, that is, except for the New York State winery laws, a body of writing in the English language that should be totally banned for having no redeeming social value.

Meanwhile, back to the Alcohol and Tobacco Tax Unit of the Internal Revenue division of the United States Treasury Department. The bond was the first thing to get, and I typed up the application myself—fool that I was. The sum was a thousand dollars, which had to be written as both "$1,000.00" and "ONE THOUSAND AND 00/100 DOLLARS." Into this latter trap I immediately blundered, and as the typewriter was in the capital position when I got to "00/100" I naturally got "))?L))." I saw this at once, went over it and mailed it in. It was promptly rejected. There can be no strikeovers on a bond application. Knowing that I was incapable of typing an application without at least one strikeover, I took the next one to a professional typist, who was so unnerved by the whole procedure that even she messed it up and I had to request a third set of blanks. Gritting her teeth, she did this one perfectly, and hurdle number one was out of the way.

The diagram and the plan were next, in other words a scale drawing of the building, its approximate location on the property, the use to which the rooms were to be put, and a separate line in a contrasting color that would separate the bonded from the nonbonded areas—those in which no wine would be produced or stored. I am no draftsman, but I had the architect's plans, a T square, drawing paper, a ruler and the knowledge of how to keep a drawing to scale. So I carefully prepared an accurately scaled drawing of the building in blue ink, and then traced over the bonded area with a red pencil. Back it came in the next mail. In the opinion of the Alcohol and Tobacco Tax Unit, blue and red are not contrasting colors. Only green and red. Nothing anywhere in the regulations says this, but there is no appeal from an ATTU ruling. So I did it again in green and red, and after a slightly longer delay it was again rejected. Points of the compass must be shown, and I had drawn an arrow indicating north—the only point required—from what my compass showed to be north. But someone in the office compared it to a geodetic survey and I was a degree or two off. Perhaps magnetic north rather than true north? So this time I copied it from the official county map, and this time it was grudgingly accepted. You will notice that so far not a word has been said about wine, and very little has ever been said in the intervening years. True north, red and green, a discrepancy of three cents in a tax return—this is what fascinates the bureaucrats. Wine? Grapes? Now does the opening section of this book begin to make sense?

This is not to be construed as an attack on a particular governmental agency, but rather as an explanation of what I call the civil service syndrome. Civil service is designed to glorify the small-minded, the man who goes by the book and who never, never thinks for himself. Thinking is the besetting sin in all government departments, nowhere more so than in a department charged with raising revenue. I worked off and on for ten years with the Voice of America, an arm of the U.S. State Department, and was therefore a federal civil service employee. And the reason this tenure was off and on was that after three or four years I was full up to here, in fact beyond here, with the awareness that it didn't matter how capable you were, how well you did your job. All that mattered was that every *i* in the book was dotted and every *t* crossed. I enjoyed directing an occasional radio program, and I resigned my full-time position and went on a part-time basis, free of the deadening influence of filing daily reports, free of the necessity of informing on one's fellow employees.

As I said, this attitude becomes particularly virulent when it involves raising revenue. I quote a story I can't vouch for, but which was told to me by the victim. A certain ATTU inspector assigned to the Finger Lakes section of New York notified the president of a large winery that his inspection had shown them to be several thousand gallons short. The president, by the way, was in bed with pneumonia and was running a temperature of 103. Such was the urgency of the demand, however, that he got out of his sickbed and, wrapped in blankets, went to the winery. A careful check showed that the winery's figures were completely accurate, whereupon the inspector laughed and said, "I just wanted to see if you knew what you were doing." For which a man's life was risked.

Every winery in the area signed a letter asking for this inspector's removal, and subsequently he was transferred. Where? To the southern district of New York, where he was promptly given a much more important post. You see, civil service likes this type of thinking, thoroughly enjoys the harassment of taxpayers. What it cannot abide is overlooking a three-cent underpayment.

A word is now due in the defense of the individual inspectors. With one or two exceptions I have found them all to be decent, cooperative men. (To this I must add "women," for I am happy to say that at the last inspection one of those delightful creatures showed up.) But their hands are tied by the book; they know that someone is looking over their shoulder. I remember one of them saying to me, "Look, I know you're going to say it's a lot of crap, and it is a lot of crap. But I've got to protect myself. If I make a mistake of ten cents some guy with an adding machine will find it, and it's my neck." The money that is spent looking for this ten cents runs into the millions. It is no coincidence that the number of heart attacks among inspectors is high. In the eighteen years that we sold wine, I worked with and got to know eight inspectors. Half of them have had coronaries, two of them fatal. I am convinced they were caused by the gnawing fear during the long hours of the night that the ten-cent error would be discovered.

On to the State of New York, a production rated "X." The State Liquor Authority is dedicated to the proposition that anyone in the wine business is a crook, and it is devoted with single-minded passion to closing up the wineries. When I went to the Authority for the first time I was shown to the desk of a man with an exalted title but very little power. In those days the hands were out in every direction, and the titles were given to political favorites to assist in their weekly collections. I said, "I would like some advice on getting into the wine business," to which he replied, "The best advice I can give you is don't get into it." This was one of the few honest answers I ever received from the SLA.

There is a vindictiveness running rampant through the state office which is lacking in the federal. Whatever harassment the ATTU inflicts on the winemaker is due more to frightened and self-protecting bureaucracy than to sheer venality. As an example, an agent will call about a form in which an error of one-tenth of a gallon shows up, and require the winemaker to file an amended copy. One-tenth of a gallon involves a tax of less than two cents. The phone call costs, say, thirty cents, a reasonably well paid clerk has spent some time checking the form to find where the error is, plus his time on the phone. The winemaker must then get his Form 702 and check it against his tax payments on Form 2050, and if the problem is still not solved he must check it against his sales invoices. Sometimes this takes the better part of an hour. Then he must call back, at another thirty cents, and explain what happened. If it was simply an error in tax payment he can remedy that at the next payment time, and there are two each month, twenty-four a year. But if it involves the "on-hand" figure, that awesome place in Form 702 where the winemaker says he has such and such a number of gallons on hand, no one at the government office may correct the figure. The winemaker must file an amended copy and pay eight cents postage to mail it. All for something involving less than two cents, which has now cost all concerned upward of ten dollars in calls, postage and time.

The State Liquor Authority is another breed altogether. A few examples will suffice. Winemakers are required to file a price schedule in twenty-five copies every month, another in twenty-five copies three times a year, and a third in one copy every other month. So some years ago I received a call in which I was told that I had failed to file. I assured my caller that I had, that I had mailed my copies in ample time to meet the tenth of the month deadline. He said, "The important thing is not whether you did or did not mail them. The important thing is that they're not on my desk." The ugly question that someone in his office had probably misfiled them was not even considered.

"What shall I do?" I said.

"If they're not on my desk by five o'clock you won't sell another bottle of wine all next month," was the reply.

The distance to their office in downtown Manhattan was thirty-five miles, and it was already after two. But I made up the twenty-five copies—which, by the way, we must pay to have printed—drove into New York City and got them to his desk at exactly five minutes to five. I thought the man was going to have apoplexy when he realized I had met his deadline. The tag line to this unfunny joke was that all the form said was "No Change in Prices."

On another occasion someone at the office was exceptionally rude over the phone, rude even for the SLA. I knew better than to do what I did, but I am a man of sudden and violent passions, and I fired off a letter in which I said that some people at the State Liquor Authority took the word "authority" too literally. In almost the next mail I received a summons to appear at the office and explain why my license shouldn't be revoked. It didn't matter on what grounds. There is no appeal from an SLA ruling. They are prosecutor, judge and jury, and I knew it. I was very active in politics at the time, and for the first and only time in my life I pulled every political string I knew and managed to keep my license.

Finally, not too long ago, I filed to raise my consumer resale prices effective July 1. The deadline for filing was May 10, and to be on the safe side I sent in the schedule on May 4 and got a "Certificate of Mailing" at the post office for my special delivery letter. They received it on May 5 at the SLA. On May 17, seven days too late to refile, they said they couldn't accept it. Oh, yes, my form was in on time. Oh, yes, they had all the information to send to the printer. What was the problem? The regulations now require the winemaker to send in price changes in triplicate, and I had sent in only one copy. In vain I said that my three previous price changes had all been submitted that way. The old answer: That was then, this is now. Anyway, the commissioner says it's time you learned how to file properly. I pointed out that I had filed at least one price schedule a month, sometimes two, and sometimes three, every month for the past eighteen years. This was the first one to be rejected. This shook him up a little, but he said, "I'm just quoting the commissioner," and hung up in my face. I should point out that this did not leave me with a serious problem. The schedule raising our prices to retailers was properly filed and accepted. It simply meant that no retailer could charge less than the old price, a hardly likely procedure when my price to them had risen by five dollars a case. They could charge as much more as the traffic would bear, but to protect my regular customers I had to send out a card to each one telling him the suggested retail price even though the official book they would receive on July 1 still listed the old price.

Back to 1952. At long last, the bond was accepted, the plan accepted, a bonded winery number had been assigned me, the state had approved my winery application, contingent on the Internal Revenue people granting me final status. Only the inspection remained, and I faced this confidently. I subsequently learned that there is never anything in the wine business to feel confident about. But this time luck was with me. An inspector named Walcott turned up to check me out, and a nicer guy it would be hard to imagine. Because of one delay or another we were now within two weeks of the beginning of the harvest, and not a drop of wine destined for commercial use could legally be made on the premises until the winery had been inspected and certified. Inspector Walcott began reading my carefully typed final application, shook his head and began to frown.

Finally he said, "Look, all of this would be all right with any normal person. But that's not the kind of person who will read it at the office. There are certain words and certain phrases that must be used. Give this to me, and I'll be back in a couple of hours."

So saying, he rolled up the papers, drove to the Internal

Revenue office in the Nyack post office, and retyped the entire application himself. When he returned he handed the papers to me to sign, and said, "These will go through. I know you can't have any delay with the grapes ripening the way they are. The whole thing's so stupid anyway."

We toasted each other in the noncommercial wine made the year before, and then he supervised my removing the remainder from what was now to be a bonded area, and in which no wine not made under the provisions of what was then known as Regulation 7 could be stored. He was about to leave when he looked in horror at the entry to the building.

"Oh, Christ," he said. "You're supposed to have a sign with letters of a certain size saying 'High Tor Vineyards—Bonded Winery #615' up on the wall outside the entrance. You have to do it." He looked at me and I heard for the first time the words I have heard so many times since. "If I say you have it up and someone comes by and finds you haven't, it's my neck."

I looked around and saw a six-foot length of board that had just been removed from a packing case. Taking a paintbrush and a can of brown deck enamel—all I could find at the moment—I lettered the magical words. I put a masonry bit in my electric drill, punched two holes in the cinder block wall, pounded in a couple of rawl plugs and mounted the sign.

"Not elegant," said the inspector, "but 'twill suffice."

"I'll have another one made in a week or so," I said, believing it.

After nineteen years the sign, like the sink and the discount-house water pump, is still there, fulfilling its federal duty. It long outlived Inspector Walcott, who was the first to go the cardiac route. Witty, intelligent and urbane, how could he possibly survive the three-tenths-of-a-gallon syndrome?

Now we were in business. It is well to remember that all we ever had in mind was being quietly permitted to make good wine, as one is quietly permitted to make a good pair of shoes if that is what one desires to do. Neither Alma nor I could conceive of the fact that although prohibition had been dead for almost twenty years, alcohol, once illegal, was in the elephantine minds of these regulatory pygmies still terribly suspect. No one (they think) would enter the wine business voluntarily unless he had a desperately illicit caper lurking just over the horizon, and by God they were going to find out what it was if only to share in the profits. Again I refer to the state, not to the federal. In all my years in this business I have never been approached by any federal inspector with anything that even smelled of a suggested kickback.

The vintage was, as I have said, less than two weeks away and we set about cleaning and sterilizing our equipment, tightening our barrels. We were not yet big enough to use anything larger than the standard fifty-gallon whiskey barrel, which in those halcyon days we could buy cleaned, steamed and freshly coopered for six dollars apiece delivered. Now they are four to six times that price.

The reason wood has played such a large role in winemaking is that wine may come in contact with very few natural materials without becoming contaminated. Iron, copper, in fact most metals, will react with the acid in the wine to make a metallic salt that will eventually cloud the wine and make it unsalable. Until the development of stainless steel and certain of the plastics, there were virtually no materials for the safe storage of wine but wood and glass, and glass had the strict practical limitation of size. So it was wood, but wood dries out when not in use, and is also an organic substance with pores and cracks where all sorts of microscopic organisms can lodge, unknown to the winemaker. All wooden containers must not only be scrupulously cleaned and sterilized prior to use, but also be tightened and filled with water until the staves swell up and hold their contents with no seepage or drip. This takes time.

Following the best practice, I had written sometime earlier to a laboratory in California for agar slants of pure wine yeast culture. This is simply a small culture medium made up of agar-agar, a gelatinous substance derived from seaweed and mixed with grape juice. A small amount of this is placed in sterilized bottles and inoculated with a carefully controlled strain of pure yeast. The home winemaker seldom does this, for grapes in the natural state contain plenty of yeast on the skin. But there are good yeasts and bad yeasts, and the winemaker has no way of knowing which will predominate unless he uses a yeast he can count on.

He starts this culture by picking a small amount of ripe grapes, squeezing them and boiling the resultant juice, killing all the wild yeasts. Then he pours the cooled juice into the pint bottle holding the culture and in a matter of hours fermentation begins. He then gets some more fresh juice, boils it, pours it into a clean gallon jug and pours the fermenting contents of the pint bottle into it. When this is fermenting heavily he repeats the process with five gallons of juice. Five gallons will start a fifty-gallon barrel, and fifty gallons will start five hundred. These larger sizes are not boiled. Happily, bad yeast is much more sensitive to sulfur dioxide than are commercial strains, and as little as 100 parts per million of sulfur dioxide (SO_2) will eliminate over 99 percent of the wild yeasts, mold and bacteria that one might expect to find in a natural juice. Incidentally, sulfur dioxide is the only chemical we used in making High Tor wine.

A day or so before the end of August I picked a small sample of the earliest variety, tested the juice for sugar with my new saccharometer and for acid with my titration outfit. Perfection. We were now ready for our first commercial vintage. It was a white variety, and white yeast culture was started with the boiled juice of that first sample I had just picked. We called our friends as we had for the private vintage of the year before, but somehow the fifteen had grown to thirty-five. And on Labor

Day weekend of 1953 we sallied forth for the first commercial harvest.

The vines being young, it was of course a small crop, but it was still the biggest by far that we had ever handled. The sugar-acid balance was just what it should have been and by the end of the day several barrels were full of the sweet, murky juice, which was then treated with SO_2. Our friends had brought a variety of food, and toward evening an impromptu picnic was held on the grass in front of the old house. The first of our many vintage parties was born.

The next morning the juice was inoculated with the furiously fermenting yeast culture and our first white wine was off to the races. Now it was time to think of the next-ripening variety, a red one.

Again I went out for the test picking, and again all was well. It was time to boil the juice and start the red wine culture. It was time, that is, but there didn't seem to be any red wine culture. I searched the place for a day, and finally asked Alma if she had seen it.

"You don't mean that empty glass bottle with the cotton in the top," she said.

"It wasn't empty," I said as a cold feeling began to haunt my lower bowel. "It had a little chunk of agar in the bottom, impregnated with wine yeast."

"My God," she said. "I thought it was something spoiled, and I threw it on the trash fire yesterday."

We poked through the ashes and came on the twisted and melted remains of a laboratory bottle, its contents scorched beyond any hope of possible resuscitation. Like any good red-blooded American male I panicked. Calls to New York winery supply houses proved fruitless. Calls to nearby wineries were also futile, as the old-fashioned native American grape they all were using at the time did not ripen for several weeks, and no one had any culture on hand that early. Then I called Phillip

Wagner and found both Phillip and Jocelyn away for the weekend. On the verge of hysteria, I called the late Herman Wente at Wente Brothers Winery in Livermore, California— my old stamping grounds. We had visited him earlier that summer and he had been, in the true wine tradition, most helpful, although I was unhappy to see the old whorehouse at Santa Rita gone. But now all I wanted was information. Mr. Wente seemed puzzled at my dilemma.

"You say you have a good white wine culture going?" he said.

"Yes. Pure Riesling wine yeast."

"Well, then, use that. It'll do the job just as well. Maybe better."

To get ahead of my story I used that yeast culture from the same laboratory in every succeeding vintage, and I wouldn't think of using anything else.

I thanked Mr. Wente profusely, kissed my wife and apologized for all the terrible things I had said, and prepared for another weekend of picking. For this we hired a couple of local housewives and three or four high school students, with my wife as chief picker and straw boss. Red wine is simpler to handle in the initial stages than white, as only crushing is required. The pressing comes later. The little crusher-stemmer we had bought in Zurich was light enough to mount directly on top of the fermenting vats. As soon as several bushel baskets were full of grapes they were loaded on a platform we had made that mounted on the back of the tractor, driven alongside the open vats and dumped directly into the crusher. This was a simple and efficient operation which we used for the next three vintages. By then the crop had become so large that bigger vats and a bigger crusher were called for, and we had to install a Moyno transfer pump to force the crushed grapes through two-inch plastic pipes to their eventual destination.

So proceeding in this fashion and picking mainly on week-ends, when we could get extra help, we brought in the entire crop. It was pitifully small, about eight hundred gallons, and I can imagine the looks of disbelief when the Alcohol and Tobacco Tax people went over the monthly reports we solemnly filed. It was no joke to us, though. We were now in business.

What were we going to call our wine? Not being thieves, we were certainly not going to steal names like Chablis, Sauternes, Rhine Wine or Burgundy, names that legitimately belong to the hard-working people who over the years have brought to the world's attention the names of the wines belonging to these clearly defined regions. I will go into this more fully later, but suffice it to say that both of us thoroughly condemn this practice, whatever the Alcohol and Tobacco Tax people, whatever the vast majority of American winemakers, may say and do.

Our grapes were grown and our wine produced in Rockland County, New York. The wine grown and produced in the Chablis district of France is called Chablis. What more natural then than to call our wines Rockland White and Rockland Red, to be followed a few years later by Rockland Rosé? This decided, we had to get a label designed. No wine may be sold until the ATTU in Washington approves a label submitted on Form 1649. Not just a sketch. A completed label containing certain clearly specified information. And this label may not be changed without subsequent resubmission of the form. A yearly sample of wine is taken at the regular inspection, and woe betide the winemaker if the sample does not agree with the information on the label. It doesn't have to be good, but it does have to agree with the label. I approve of this.

With much trepidation we approached a neighbor, the well-known artist Henry Varnum Poor. Would he, under the wildest set of circumstances, even consider designing a label? We knew, of course, of his interest in High Tor. He was delighted with the idea, and then we approached the thorny subject of price. He replied, quite seriously, that we could not possibly afford what he would have to charge on a commercial basis. When he saw our lengthening faces he laughed and said, "So why not just settle for a case or two of wine a year?" We shook hands on that and the bargain was sealed. Until his death in December of 1970 we brought him wine, although I am afraid that in the press of business or personal problems an occasional delivery was omitted. Henry, wherever you are, forgive us.

When the design was completed he signed it with his regular signature: "H. V. Poor." Thus it is that we have probably the only signed wine label in the world. Sample labels were run at a specialty printing house in New York, and when everyone was satisfied with the final result, we glued it to Form 1649 and with crossed fingers dispatched it to Washington. Strange to say, it was approved at the first submission, and we were ready to offer the wine for sale in New York.

By now I am sure you will believe me when I say that this was not a simple matter. A price had to be established, and considerably prior to placing it on the market, price schedules—twenty-five of one, twenty-five of another, one of this, two of that—had to be filed. And now it suddenly dawned on us that we had no idea what to charge for our wine. Wagner again. What was he getting retail in that far-off year of 1954? One dollar and a half a bottle, he replied. Fine. That sounds like a good price. And on that scientific piece of market research we established our first bottle price.

4

This is as good a place as any to go into the difference between the making and aging of white wine and red wine. Red wine, as I've said earlier, is fermented "on the skins" to extract the color. Most red grapes have a white pulp; color exists only in the skins. It is quite possible to crush and press most varieties of red grapes, ferment the clear juice and come up with a white wine. Much of the great French champagne is made from Pinot noir, a red grape responsible for all the great red Burgundies of the Côte d'Or. In the second case the pulp is fermented in contact with the skins, and as the alcohol develops it extracts the color pigments from the skins until they are all in solution in the fermenting juice. In making white wine one takes the grapes, either white or red, crushes and presses them, and ferments the juice much as one does in making hard cider. When the fermentation is complete, the sediment falls to the bottom of the container, and gradually the wine becomes clear.

The great majority of the thinking today is that light, fresh white wines do not benefit by aging. The wines of Alsace and of the Loire Valley, among others, are bottled as soon as they are candle bright—a candle held behind a container of wine will show the sharp edges of the flame clearly defined. It is also true that white wine in this category is better off for never having seen wood. Wood is semiporous, and an exchange between the wine and the air outside begins a slow process of oxidation. But oxidation is the absolute enemy of white wines, for it deepens and yellows the wine and in a light white table wine this is a disaster. It is no coincidence that most homemade wines are red. They are hard to spoil and a reasonable amount of oxidation is all to the good. But it requires considerable know-how to make a light, fruity, brilliantly clear white table wine.

With all this in mind we had determined to bottle our white wine not later than June first of the following year, preferably in May. It would then have to age at least two months in the bottle before going on the market. The red wine we had decided to bottle at eighteen months to two years. So July 1 of 1954 was the date we aimed at to bring the first of the 1953 Rockland White on the market. That meant that the Minimum Consumer Resale Prices had to be posted by May 10, and the prices to retailers by June 10. *Mirabile dictu,* as I believe the saying goes, all this happened with no flak from anyone. If we could figure a simple way of sticking on the labels and folding the foil cap around the neck of the bottles we would be able to offer our first wine on the market. Four and a half years after acquiring High Tor we would receive our first return.

Bottles we bought in those early innocent days from a "used bottle dealer"—i.e., a junkman in Brooklyn. It is legal to use wine bottles over and over again, although illegal for spirits. In these days of ecological recycling I can see absolutely no reason why this ban against the reuse of spirit bottles should be allowed to continue. The used bottle comes from the dealer in sparkling and immaculate condition and it is simply insane to ban the use of whiskey bottles for a second, third, even tenth time except to keep a good thing going for the glassmakers.

We were bottling a quality wine, so the decision was made at an early stage to use corks instead of plastic or screw-cap stoppers. Cork still offers a certain advantage to a wine that is to be given some bottle age, for it allows a transfer of air between the wine and the outside atmosphere. But cork can be an enormous nuisance if it is not good cork, and we were well aware of this fact. A porous, spongy cork will deteriorate rapidly and give the wine a moldy taste. It will also split when a short corkscrew is driven through it, leaving the lower half in the bottle defying all attempts to evict it short of driving it in. Finally, we had the choice of lead, aluminum or plastic caps to put over the corks. Plastic is the easiest to use and also the worst looking. Of the other two lead is the easiest to handle with inexpensive machinery, so we chose it. Everybody relax. The lead caps stay firmly on the *outside* of the bottle and cannot in any way contribute to lead poisoning. It is, perhaps, one of the better ways to use lead.

Where do you get the corks? Would you believe that the Armstrong Cork Company, which got its start in the closure business, still maintains a small but active business in wine corks? When one of their salesmen came to see me I laughed and said I was only interested in ten thousand corks, and I couldn't believe this would be of any interest to them. Imagine my surprise to have him tell me that this was well within their range and that they would be happy to fill my order. I wound up ordering "extra first" inch-and-a-half corks. They proved not long enough and I later bought inch-and-three-quarters. I might add that I stopped buying them from Armstrong, even though I never got a bad cork from them. But a man came along who almost depended on the business, his corks were just as good, and the price was right. Armstrong, I am sorry. But I felt you could survive without me.

The caps were easier. As the background color of our white label was gold, we chose a silver foil cap, which we applied with a $3.50 rubber-jawed capper. I was warned by my supplier that this machine was of American manufacture and therefore would not last. I should add that this supplier was solidly Prussian and literally spit out the word "American." But like so many other things we bought in this age of so-called planned obsolescence, it is still in use. Could the real fault lie in the fact that so many Americans don't take care of their possessions?

Getting the labels on the bottles, however, presented a much more challenging problem. We used a front and a back label then—we used only the front label subsequently—and each one had to be properly aligned and had to stick at the first application. Further, as wine bottles are frequently immersed in ice buckets, we had to use a water-resistant glue. This rules out much of the more readily available glue, and many water-resistant glues do not immediately adhere on contact. Of course regular labeling glues are available, but only in the larger-size drums. Five gallons was the smallest size we could get, and invariably the last two or three gallons dried out before we could finish the drum and had to be discarded. Finally we tried Elmer's Glue, and though it was not as "instant stick" as we would have liked, it was water-resistant and with a little patience did the job. We used it for about fifteen years, buying it in the one-gallon size. The labels were run through a rebuilt Potdevin electric label gummer, which left a thin coat of glue on the back. Then they were slapped on the bottle by hand and held for a few seconds until the glue set. You can see why we discarded the back labels.

Finally it was July 1, 1954, and we were ready to sell. I climbed into our brand-new station wagon, "High Tor Vineyards" emblazoned on the front doors, and started to make the rounds of the stores. I am not a salesman and hate to sell, but I was amazed at the response we got. Here was a totally new product, made in an area where wine had never been made commercially before, but almost every liquor store I visited ordered at least one case. (In New York, wine can be sold only in liquor stores or in restaurants. Why this should be in the second-largest wine-producing state in the country I have no idea. Considering the importance of the wine industry to the state, one would think it could be sold at groceries and supermarkets along with the food it is to accompany, but of course this would be much too sensible.)

I returned that night after having visited seventeen liquor stores and got orders from fifteen of them. What a snap, we both thought. At that rate we would be on a paying basis in no time at all. Alas for the dreams of youth.

In those halcyon days the wine tax was paid by simply sticking a stamp on the case, a supremely simple operation for the small winemaker. I can, however, realize the objections the bulk wineries had about keeping thousands of dollars tied up in stamps which had to be on hand before the wine was even sold. For us it was simplicity itself. We would go to the Internal Revenue office in New York City, buy a sheet of one hundred stamps for $40.80, and our next one hundred cases were tax paid through the simple process of affixing one stamp to each case. More recently we would pay twice a month, from the first to the fifteenth, and from the sixteenth to the end of the month. We made up these tax payments—Form 2050—in quadruplicate, sending three copies to a gentleman named FitzGerald at the IRS center in New York and one copy to the Assistant Regional Commissioner, Alcohol, Tobacco Tax and Firearms. Further, we could not incur a tax liability of over one hundred dollars in any two-week period without filing for a special bond. And these forms must be filed whether any wine is sold or not, and every day during the period must be accounted for. And if you sell only one case of wine during the period you must still accompany the form with a check for forty-one cents. I could suggest how the government could save millions of dollars a year, but then who would listen?

Meanwhile, back at the winery, Alma and I got the first orders together. We sat up late packing the cases, wrapping each bottle in tissue paper, a practice we abandoned when we discovered that the liquor store owners considered it a nuisance, promptly stripped it all off and threw it out. We made out the invoices, which by State Liquor Authority ruling must be serially prenumbered and bound in pads so that each can be accounted for, and which must consist of an original and a "true duplicate" in different color, which duplicate must be kept on the premises available at any time to a hungry state inspector.

This done, we applied the stamps and moved the wine into the tax-paid room, as only wine in bond may be kept on a bonded premises. And finally, all governmental requirements having been met, we slept, dreaming of the unquestionable affluence that so soon must be ours.

The first orders were delivered, a deep breath taken, and I hit the road again. Not quite so much success this time, for I had called on the best stores first. Still, not bad. The local restaurants we frequented were called on, and all of them ordered. What we didn't know was that some of these restaurants would make an expensive visit to their place a requisite to a reorder, and if we wanted to sell a second case at twelve dollars we had to spend upward of twenty dollars on dinner for the order. These "customers" we long ago gave up.

What really sobered us and ended our dreams of instant riches was my first sales trip across the river into Westchester County. Not only did I not sell a single case, I was practically given the bum's rush out of store after store. Who wants to buy a wine named "Rockland White"? What's that mean on a label? Nothing, that's what. Call it Chablis, or Rhine Wine, or Sauterne, or any of the names people know, and we'll talk to you. But not at $1.50 a bottle. How can a little winery make good wine? Everyone knows that the best wine is made by the biggest winemakers. And on and on. When looking for a place to move to from the city we had always resisted Westchester. Now I was beginning to understand why.

Consider this whole business of label names. For reasons never clearly understood by me our government permits the theft of names that legitimately belong to someone else. "Champagne" is the most notorious example. In France no sparkling wine can be called champagne unless made from certain grapes, grown in a tightly controlled district and made by the bottle fermentation process. (Champagne is made from finished white wine which undergoes a secondary fermentation in a sealed bottle, so that the carbon dioxide given off through the fermentation process does not escape but remains trapped in the form of bubbles. Another method is to produce this secondary fermentation in stainless steel pressure tanks and then bottle the sparkling wine like soda pop. This is a distinctly inferior method and all sparkling wine made that way must be labeled "Bulk Process" or "Charmat Process." Because this process was developed in France many American winemakers say on their labels "Made by the French Charmat Process," and innocent American buyers assume that means the real way to make it. Our government condones this.)

Most countries respect the label laws of other countries. Sparkling wine made in Germany is called "Sekt"; in Italy it is "Spumanti." In a famous recent court case something called "Spanish Champagne" was being sold in England. The French Champagne makers brought suit and won and the product had to be withdrawn from the market. But in this country any sparkling white wine that has not been artificially carbonated can be called champagne, provided it is made from grapes. Any grapes, made by anyone, anywhere. I was told by someone in a position to know that when Thompson seedless grapes are laid out to be dried into raisins they can withstand one or two rains. But if it rains enough to place them in imminent danger of spoiling they are gathered up and made into "champagne." In

73

New York I have tasted champagnes sweetened with Concord grape concentrate that tastes like sparkling bubble gum.

This situation applies to all famous European area names. Chablis is not a wine type, it is a small geographical area in France and only wine made there from certain specific grapes should be so labeled. The same is true of Burgundy, as it is true of Sauternes—with or without the final *s*. In this connection it is interesting to know that in France "Haute Sauternes" describes wine made in the upper Sauternes. In California it means sweeter than "regular" sauterne, and is universally pronounced "hot saw-tern."

But if ever a geographical term was misused it is "Rhine Wine." Most Americans don't know that Champagne, Chablis, Burgundy and Sauternes are regional names and as such have a specific meaning in their own country. But every American knows all about the Rhine, and to tolerate a California or New York wine bearing the label "Rhine Wine" is disgraceful. Perhaps the maddest label I have ever seen—and I don't mean to put down Widmer's, because they're a good outfit—said "Widmer's Neapolitan Brand New York State Rhine Wine."

A relative few in this field escaped such piracy by banding together early and spending money on court cases to defend their exclusive right to certain names. "Cognac" may not be infringed upon, nor may "Scotch." In the field of cheese "Roquefort" is protected. But these are isolated examples and simply point up the fact that it should not be necessary to protect what is rightfully yours. Can one imagine the furor if there suddenly appeared on the market something called "Olde Missionary Brand Genuine Vermont Maple Syrup—Product of South Africa"? Or "Pilsudski Brand Genuine Virginia Smithfield Ham—Produced & Packed in Poland"? Yet that's what we're doing.

American winemakers are not alone in this thievery. Denmark is if anything worse. "Real Danish Camembert"? Real

74

Camembert comes from France. "Danish Fontina"? Fontina comes from Italy. Gouda, Port Salud, Swiss. And the sad part of it is that none of it's any good. I have long suspected that the Danes maintain a huge secret factory somewhere in which enormous quantities of flavorless orange-colored "cheese" is made. This flows in a continuous glutinous stream to various different-shaped molds labeled "Fontina," "Fynboe," "Gouda," "Port Salud," where it is encased in a cherry-red waxy plastic and shipped to the far reaches of the world as real this and genuine that. And the plague is spreading. Recently I saw in a supermarket an item labeled "Imported Swiss Cheese." In microscopic letters it also said "Product of Austria." If ever there was a label designed to mislead the public this was it, but it's all legal.

The villain in most of these cases is the word "imported." What does "imported" actually mean? It means that someone in another country can produce something cheaper than you can, and it's worth his time financially to ship it out. "Scotch whisky" is by law made in Scotland, so why does it have to say "imported"? The same is true of Canadian whisky. The magic word appears on the label only for the purpose of implying that anything worth importing must be superior. Yet many imported items are imported for price alone, and frequently are dumped here after they have failed to sell in their own country. Beaujolais is a classic example. The French will drink it only when it's young, knowing that it does not age well. So after a batch of Beaujolais passes the point where no discerning Frenchman will drink it, it is shipped here and sold as "Rare Old Beaujolais—Imported."

As I write this on a hot afternoon in July there is an open bottle of Heineken beer beside the typewriter. It says in large letters, "Brewed in Holland." Why does it need the word "Imported" on the neck label? How could it possibly have got within my reach if it were not imported? If there were one word that I could expunge from the labels of products sold in America, that word would be "imported."

Incidentally, if you want to put down one of your British friends—and they all need putting down every so often—you can tell him that bourbon was a civilized and accepted drink almost one hundred years before Scotch. Inasmuch as all Britons insist that anything called "whisky" with no qualifying description is Scotch, and the others are Johnny-come-latelies, it should be enlightening for them to learn that bourbon was more or less settled into its present formula in the 1780s in Bourbon County, Kentucky. As such it was "imported" by the British, as Scotch was still a rough, tough peasant drink made in the Highlands of Scotland over a pot still. Not until the invention of the "Patent Still" in the 1870s did the Scots learn how to blend their popskull down with neutral spirits to the point where anyone but a Highlander could touch it. In fact, it was not until a lawsuit in 1905 that the definition of Scotch whisky was clearly established. By that time bourbon had been made under the same formula for almost one hundred and twenty-five years.

If you really want to madden the British wait until you hear one carrying on about the "American sweet tooth." When he has finished you can casually tell him that the average Englishman consumes vastly more sugar than does the average American. Official figures compiled by the sugar industry itself show that America is not even second behind England, but ranks fairly well down on the list.

To return to the use of the word "imported," it has always seemed insane to me that we should have to import foreign names and titles to describe something made in this country. This was not always true in eastern America, when a sparkling wine from the Catawba grape was sold under that name, and hotelkeepers were accused of passing off inferior French champagne when a guest ordered "Sparkling Catawba." But all that has changed over the years. Chablis made in the Chablis district of France must be the standard of excellence for any wine so labeled. It may be possible to produce in California a white wine labeled Chablis that is better than the best of the originals, but it can never be a better Chablis, just as a car made in Japan can never be a better Buick. It may be a better car, but never a better Buick, because that name belongs to General Motors, and anything else called a Buick can only be an imitation. With our vast winemaking potential and our skills, why must we be imitators?

The same is true of cheese. There are "Swiss" cheeses made in Ohio and Wisconsin that even the Swiss grudgingly admit they cannot tell from their own. But Swiss is Swiss is Swiss is Swiss, and anything else made under that name is derivative. I have been served on the Cunard Line, of all places, a Brie made in Illinois as good as any Brie I have ever tasted, but it can still never be any better than a copy. Even Borden, I almost hesitate to say, puts out a Camembert that is infinitely better than any "imported" canned Camembert on the market, whether it is imported from Denmark or indeed France.

My question is why can't all this expertise go into the development of cheeses or wines that can stand on their own feet? Liederkranz is wholly American, and it has never had to lean on someone else's name. Gold 'n Rich, not one of the world's great cheeses to be sure but still adequate, gets by on not only an American name, but a folksy one to boot. In this connection it has always seemed strange that spelling something wrong or slipping into the most uneducated of vernaculars is supposed to make something taste better. "Chicken 'n Basket," "Franks 'n Beans." On one page of the food supplement of a recent local paper I see "Finger Lickin' Good," "Ham 'n Swiss," "Puddin' 'n Pie." How much more character would an English-style steak house have had if it had been called "The Coach and Four" instead of its actual title, "Coach 'n Four"? It sounds as though the stableman himself were running it.

This carries over into the wines. I think I've belabored sufficiently the Chablis-Sauternes-Burgundy syndrome, but what about the varietals? If Pinot noir produces the great red Burgundies of the Côte d'Or, and fifty miles to the south produces a second-rate wine, what will guarantee that it will produce a superior wine seven thousand miles away in California? Cabernet Sauvignon, the basic ingredient of the great wines of the Médoc, makes quite a different wine in as nearby a district as Pomerol, an altogether different wine in Chile, and something else again in California. The fact that California in my opinion comes the closest to emulating its great model in the Médoc of any Cabernets grown anywhere is purely coincidental. It is still a different wine and should be named for the district in which it grows. There is no need for Château Margaux or Château Lafite Rothschild to have anything but the maker's name and the district on the label. American wines will not come of age until the same thing applies here.

Despite the setback in Westchester County, I still managed to sell more wine than we made, and right after Christmas of 1954 we were totally out of wine. This was not a happy experience, for it meant we would have nothing to market until the following June. Nineteen fifty-four was a large vintage, and we would have a lot more white wine. This was a mixed blessing, for the public is fickle and has a great tendency to say five months later, "High Tor what?" Also, the 1953 red would be ready, a wine that was as yet untried commercially. So the winter and early spring of 1955 were full of foreboding, and the steady wrangles with officialdom were almost welcome as a diversion. On top of all this I had developed bursitis, and on New Year's Eve of 1955 had four large calcium deposits removed from my right shoulder. Forgetting the date in my discomfort, I had called the doctor late in the afternoon to see if I could have it done the next morning. Thinking it over, he decided he would probably feel better early New Year's Eve than on New Year's morning, so I was probably the only patient at New York's huge Presbyterian Hospital having an elective operation at 9 P.M. on New Year's Eve.

It was a minor operation, but it hampered me considerably over the next month or so. We have always used a hand corker, where one sits astride a bench and places a full bottle on a little platform in front of the operator. A cork which has been soaked in hot water to soften it is placed in a slot and a large lever is pulled forward, compressing the cork between two rollers until it is smaller around than the neck of the bottle. Then an iron rod pushes the compressed cork down into the bottle, where it springs back to its normal size to fit tightly against the inside of the neck. This lever requires quite a pull, and as it is mounted on the right-hand side, that of my troublesome shoulder, our bottling was severely delayed. Fortunately, we had no large tanks at that time, which would have had to be emptied all on one day. We relied entirely on fifty-gallon barrels in those long-ago days, and as each barrel contained approximately 250 bottles, one barrel was about as much as my shoulder could take at one sitting. The bottles were stood upright for twenty-four hours to allow the corks to set, after which they were laid on their sides in bins to keep the corks from drying out and letting air in to spoil the wine.

During the long cold months we got it all bottled, and Alma and I packed it away in bins holding 2,500 bottles each, or a little over two hundred cases. On June 1 it was ready for market.

The summer of 1955 saw the first major expansion of our facilities. We had four seven-hundred-gallon casks built for us by an aged Italian cooper in lower Manhattan. They were made of white oak sawed up from larger casks that this enterprising gentleman had bought from bankrupt wineries, and thus they did not have to be seasoned as new oak would. They were built to fit an exact space in the winery, and were of a size that would permit their being moved in through the big double doors intact. These casks solved the immediate storage problems.

But our biggest investment was a Willmes press, made in Germany and considered to be the first basic improvement in wine presses since biblical times. I had read about it and seen pictures, and finally I decided that we must have one. I believe ours was the second or third in this country. Now everyone has them who can afford them.

It was easy to want one, but hard to find out how to get it. I called my Prussian supplier in the city, and that wily and extremely elderly gentleman did his best to talk me out of it. He was peddling a continuous press, the sort of thing one uses when one is making bulk wine by the million gallons. I explained I wasn't making bulk wine, but he brushed me aside.

"It hass two zpigots. Goot vine comes from vun, und bum vine from ze ozzer."

In vain I said that I didn't make any "bum vine." It's American, isn't it? he answered. The Willmes press is too expensive to use for anything but good wine. German wine. Finally, when he realized I was adamant, he said he would see what he could do. What I didn't know was that his company didn't have the franchise to import the press into the country, and I was unprepared for the scheme he came up with a day or two later. He would order one to be shipped to Chile, but when the boat stopped at Cuba (this was before Castro) it would be unloaded there. Then it would be "imported" (there's that word again) from Cuba into Florida, and from there sent to New York by freight.

This all seemed so preposterous that I decided to think it over for a while. By the sheerest coincidence I was talking to a man the very next day who told me that the Willmes franchise was held by a winery equipment firm in Egg Harbor, New Jersey. A quick phone call established this fact, and also that if I got a deposit to them the press would be on its way within a matter of days. I picked the smallest model, the price for which was $3,500, and sent off the check. A few days later I received a phone call saying that the press was being loaded aboard ship in Hamburg the following day. I could forget about the press that had the spigot for taking off the "bum vine."

What was so different about this press that I went to such trouble and expense to get one? Listen. The Willmes Presser, to give it its exact name, is a long, ribbed cylinder which acts as a bracing for a sleeve of stainless steel. The sleeve is perforated with myriads of slits, big enough for juice to pass through but too small for seeds and bits of stem. Inside this sleeve is a heavy rubber sack that runs the length of the cylinder. Through three removable doors the cylinder is filled with crushed grapes, and the doors are replaced and securely locked. Then the rubber sack is inflated with compressed air, and as it enlarges like a giant balloon it forces the crushed grapes against the sleeve. The juice runs out through the slits and is collected in a pan slung beneath the press, where it is pumped off to its eventual destination. The air is then released, a switch is flipped and the cylinder revolves, breaking up the pomace (the winemaker's term for crushed grape) into new patterns. The sack is inflated again to a slightly higher pressure, and this process is continued, never allowing the pomace to cake into a solid pattern and impede the flow. In a conventional hydraulic press the juice in the center has several feet to travel, and as these presses build up tremendous pressures much of the juice is trapped and lost. With the Willmes the juice never has more than a few inches to go, and as the pomace is broken up between each pressing all the juice is extracted at a pressure that never exceeds ninety pounds. If it does, a safety valve opens with a blast of sound that will ensure that an operator will never let it happen a second time. And as the pressing medium is rubber it does not crush seeds or bits of stem, which would release excess tannin into the wine. Almost best of all, when the pressing is done and the pomace tumbled for the last time, the doors can be removed and the residue, by now almost as dry as sawdust, dumped into the pan hanging underneath. The pan is unhooked from the press and rolled on its own casters to wherever the refuse is being collected, rinsed off with a hose, rolled back and hooked in place. And all of this by one solitary man. I do not believe we could have operated the winery the way we did without this press. The original rubber sack lasted for ten years, and the second has been in use for seven. A third is waiting in the winery.

Getting it set up, however, was not all beer and skittles. It weighed almost a ton, and as the trailer truck that brought it could not get up our hill we had to transfer it into our small pickup down on the road, after which the truck driver waved cheerily and drove off, leaving me and one helper to unload it. We did it, but almost killed ourselves in the process. Then we found that all the motors were industrial and operated on three-phase electricity. The nearest three-phase was over a mile away, and the utility company wanted two thousand dollars to bring it up to us. So I bought a three-phase twelve-thousand-watt generator for six hundred dollars which runs off the power take-off of my tractor. With enormous help from friends in the local union of the International Brotherhood of Electrical Workers, everything was finally set up and running a scant two days before the 1955 vintage was to begin.

(While instructions for the press itself came in English, those for the air compressor were in the most involved and convoluted German. The German farmer I had working for me couldn't begin to read it, and I took it to a knowledgeable East Prussian couple who lived a little way down the hill. Imagine my surprise when the husband couldn't read it either, so elegant and scientific was the idiom. But his wife had gone to college, and she could make it out. She knew nothing of machinery but her husband did, so she would translate from fancy German into simple German. He would look at the drawings, say "Ah, zo," and translate it into English, which I wrote down for the future use of the almost 100 percent Italian membership of the IBEW who were to set it up.

(As for the generator, in addition to three-phase it contained taps for 110–220 volt regular house current. We ran an underground line up to the house and connected it into the regular service with a two-way switch which would make it impossible to send our current out over the line to electrocute a lineman working on a broken wire. Many times we have been grateful that the utility company's stiff demands forced us to buy the generator, never more so than during the big blackout of 1965, when our house was ablaze with light, the water pump, the refrigerator and the freezer running normally, with enough power left over to use one oven or two top burners on the electric stove.)

The 1955 vintage was the first in which the vines could be expected to give something like a maximum yield. But nothing in the grape business ever goes exactly as planned, and 1955 was no exception. Grapes are fickle things, yielding heavily when least expected and giving heartbreakingly small crops with as little reason. I have always felt that all objects, inanimate as well as animate, have wills of their own, and none has a stronger will than does a grapevine. Also, they are preyed upon by countless insects and diseases and must be catered to and coddled like veritable hypochondriacs. They are almost the only fruit that cannot successfully be grown by the organic method alone, and I say this fully aware that I will be ruffling some purist feathers. But raised in areas where disease exists—and it exists anywhere that wild grapes grow—they must be sprayed or dusted if one is to get a crop.

When speaking of phylloxera in an earlier chapter I pointed out that this scourge was America's gift to Europe. But we also gave them much more: black rot, brown rot, powdery mildew, downy mildew, dead arm disease and others. Now Europe is giving us some in return, the virus diseases, as an example, which have run rampant through France, and from there got to California. Through the most strenuous of efforts they have not as yet obtained a real foothold in New York.

Grapes grew in Europe for centuries free of disease. This was not because they were grown without the use of chemical fertilizers but because there were no diseases present. In the forests of eastern America the wild grapes are riddled with disease even while growing in the most natural and organic of conditions. Deep in the woods one will find vines growing beneath ancient and healthy beeches, maples and hemlocks, their roots buried under the accumulated years of natural leaf mold, yet still so diseased with the various fungus afflictions that they cannot ripen their grapes more than one year out of five. And if wild vines suffer so badly think of the susceptibility of varieties that never had to contend with these conditions during their own evolutionary process. It is much the same as measles wiping out the population of the South Sea islands, or the common cold proving fatal to certain primitive peoples when they were first exposed to it.

No, disease spreads because people spread it. Whether Columbus's sailors brought venereal disease back to Europe is problematical, but the great and deadly sweep of syphilis through western Europe would seem to indicate that they did. The giant African snails were brought to Florida by a young boy as pets for his grandmother, Dutch elm blight was transmitted by a furniture manufacturer. With the ever-increasing rate of rapid and worldwide travel, who can say that a man walking through an upland field in central Africa might not pick up on his shoes some parasite that the local grass has hosted harmlessly for centuries, then a few days later walk through a Dutch tulip field where a stray parasite or two falls off into the dirt. And supposing this interloper now discovers that it likes tulips far better than Pangola Grass, yet tulips have no resistance? There goes the tulip industry. The organic gardeners will shake their heads and say it was all brought about through the use of Chilean nitrate.

Let me make it clear that I am by no means putting down organic gardening as such. I am saying, however, that it is not the entire answer to all the ills of agriculture. Certainly a plant raised on natural fertilizer the way nature intended it to be will tend to be healthier than a plant hypoed into excess growth through the use of overdoses of nitrate, and this healthier plant will certainly throw off diseases better than the latter. But just as smallpox will overcome the healthiest man, certain diseases will overcome the healthiest plant, and if vaccination is necessary for the man, spraying is necessary for the plant.

Again, I am not making a case for the indiscriminate use of chemicals and additives. The list of "materials" authorized for use in wine at the beginning of this book states my position on that. But not all synthetics are necessarily bad, and not all natural things are good. Looking out the window right now I can see poison ivy, and I can see deadly nightshade, two of nature's children that are best avoided by man. If I crane my neck a little I can see a sassafras bush, the roots of which for many generations were used to flavor "old-fashioned," "natural" root beer. A few years ago it was discovered that the oil obtained from sassafras roots was in fact a carcinogen, and its use was banned. Now all root beer is artificially flavored, and while it doesn't taste quite as good, at least it doesn't give you cancer.

The above polemic out of the way, let me return to 1955. One of our red varieties, S. 7053, is unusually susceptible to downy mildew, and also was rather badly burned by Bordeaux mixture, the only spray that then seemed to control it. So rather rashly I switched to one of the newer sprays, Ferbam, a product that is now known to be very effective against black rot, but which simply waves cheerily to mildew and goes on its way. The result was that the entire crop of this red mainstay was lost.

In later years we sprayed with Captan for downy mildew and black rot, Karathane for powdery mildew, and Sevin for insects, and all was well. But that early in the game the loss of the heaviest-producing red variety we had appeared to us a disaster, and partly led to an unfortunate decision I will go into later. Everything else, however, went well, and we were thankful that we had the extra cooperage, and particularly thankful for the press.

We were still living in West Nyack and commuting daily to High Tor, but early in 1956 we finally recognized the fact that we couldn't run the winery with our collective left hand, that I would have to get out of the radio business and devote full time to High Tor. That being the case, it seemed foolish to have an adequate house on the premises and not use it. With a sense of regret we decided to sell the Victorian house on the millpond, the house with the twenty-five-by-forty-foot living room and the twelve-foot ceilings. We had all had some wonderful times there in the nine years we had owned it, but business, after all, is business. A real estate broker found us a buyer, and just as we were on the point of signing a contract my mother suddenly decided that she wanted it. It was a major league dilemma, but blood is thicker than brokerage—even thicker when there's no brokerage—and we let my mother have it. The agent still grumbles about it when our paths occasionally cross.

The reason my mother wanted it leads directly into another bizarre story. A few years earlier the supposedly final route of the New York Thruway was published, and the ominous black line ran about one hundred yards from our house, and directly over my mother's house a half mile away. I called Steve Doig, our lawyer and the justice of the peace, and proposed that we go to Albany and protest what amounted to concentrating the full power of the state on two members of a single family. At the very least it was un-American. Always happy to go to Albany

86

(he was finally to get there as an assemblyman), Steve agreed, and we saw all the pirates who were then riding high under the administration of Thomas E. Dewey, and who are now riding even higher. Steve was superb and almost brought tears to *my* eyes. But the one who cried in the final analysis was our legal beagle himself, for when the new plans came out the Thruway was moved from our house a half mile over to his house. We have often discussed what would have been an adequate fee for having the Thruway moved from a client's house to his attorney's. Where his house once stood is now about halfway between exits 12 and 13.

We were now untouched in any way by the concrete monster, but in curving back toward the original route it missed my mother's house by only about a hundred yards. At first it wasn't so bad but as more and more tandem trucks and buses began pounding up the long incline, and as my mother advanced into her seventies, it became intolerable, hence the desire to move to a familiar house, a house she felt at home in.

With the decision to move full time to High Tor came the necessity of enlarging the old house. We had never used it for anything but rough living, and many of the bathroom appliances described earlier were still in use. Indeed, we were still going from the first floor to the second by means of a ladder. All this was a golden opportunity for Alma, a compulsive builder, to sink her teeth into something. I used to say that if she had her way the house would ascend in tiers to the top of the mountain, while I descended in tears to the bottom. A new room was added, doubling the size of the living room, which, now being three steps higher than the addition, became the dining room. The ladder was replaced by a set of stairs, steep to be sure, but stairs nonetheless. The downstairs bathroom, which had started life as a woodshed, was completely remodeled, and the old tin shower gave way to a bathtub, while upstairs another bathroom was added with a stall shower. The whole thing was capped off with a large wooden deck on two sides of the new living room.

All this only whetted Alma's appetite, but as we had by now gone through the lion's share of the money we had got for selling the old house, I cried "Enough." Anyway, the 1956 vintage was coming on apace, and it was a vintage I will never forget. What we had hoped for in 1955 came through in spades in 1956. In all my years at High Tor I never saw a heavier crop, and in my inexperience I had no idea then of its true dimension. Wires were stretching and pulling loose as the grapes swelled to the bursting point. The last three weeks were hot and dry and the grape sugar developed almost to the point of syrup. Labor Day finally arrived, and as usual we held a vintage party and invited our friends to come and help with the first day's picking. A barrel of wine was set out under the trees, and the guests brought food for a buffet table. If the Internal Revenue is reading this let me say that the wine was tax paid before removal from the winery.

These vintage parties had by now settled into a regular pattern. Starting with the thirty-five guests at the first one, the number had grown at an ever increasing rate until by 1956 we were hosting perhaps 125. It was by invitation only, and each guest brought a casserole or, if single, potato chips, cookies or whatever. Then each was given a pair of grape-picking shears and some bushel baskets, and sent into the field being picked that day. As the cold wine in the barrel was slowly but steadily transferred into the pickers the pace slackened until by mid-afternoon the grapes were sent to the press and the ladies present began bringing out the casseroles which had been heating in relays in the kitchen. Then everyone ate, slept on the grass, or sang. The more conscientious guests helped in picking up the paper cups and plates, the few who had underestimated the strength of the wine were poured into their cars, the inevitable stuck car or two was pulled out of the ditch, and it was over. As I say, that was the way it normally went.

Nineteen fifty-six, however, was such a favorable year that the picking had actually begun several days before Labor Day, and a fair amount of juice was already bubbling away inside the winery, which, as it turned out, was just as well. For shortly after the festivities began full bushel baskets of grapes began appearing at the crusher at shorter and shorter intervals, and it soon became apparent that they were coming in faster than the crusher and the press could handle them. I sent word back to slow down, but everyone was so carried away by the joys of the vintage and the quantities of chilled white wine available for drinking that the order was ignored. At the end of the day when the last truckload was brought down someone mumbled something about more baskets being up in the field, which I took to mean ten or fifteen. Never mind, I said, I'll get them in the morning. The last load went in the press and was pumped away, the equipment was washed down, the last remaining guests had a nightcap, and the eventful day was over.

Somehow, though, I had a foreboding that all was not right. The sugar was so high that it was an unusually hot fermentation. (In addition to alcohol and carbon dioxide being created through fermentation, a considerable amount of heat is generated which, unless kept under control, can spoil the wine.)

After eating a late supper I decided to spend the night in the winery, where I could keep a close watch on things. Regularly throughout the night I got up and took the temperature of the wine, attempting to cool it as best I could by running streams of cold water over the casks and barrels. But the feeling of foreboding would not go away, and finally at four-thirty I got up, dressed, mounted the tractor and went up to see just how many grapes had not been brought down. And what to my wondering eyes did appear? Not Saint Nicholas. Just 240 full bushel baskets of grapes—about six tons. I was all alone. Even at that early hour the promise of another hot day could be felt, and if the grapes were not processed immediately the hot sun would start them fermenting in the baskets and they would be ruined. I went back to the winery and thought about it awhile. Finally I decided to call for help. Two friends responded, Herb Stever and Paul Miner, two of nature's noblemen if ever that phrase was valid. Showing up shortly after eight, they stayed until after dark, and among us all the grapes were picked up and carted down, their juice safely bedded down to begin its arduous transformation into wine.

It was a monumental vintage, and when it was over I had exactly one empty fifty-gallon barrel in the winery. Wine must be "racked," that is, pumped off into clean containers to clear it of its sediment. I couldn't do this until I bottled enough wine to have sufficient empty containers to rack the new wine into. While I am on the subject of sediment let me clear up some common misconceptions. Sediment is a natural by-product of wine, being nothing more or less than dead yeast cells and bits of grape solid that fall to the bottom. Much of it is eliminated by racking, as the wine is pumped through a hose that is not inserted all the way to the bottom of the barrel and thus handles only the relatively clear wine. If this is repeated several times the wine is clear and bright to the naked eye. But microscopic amounts remain, which in the past were accepted. The reason for the push-up or deep indentation in the bottom of older wine bottles is not to make them stronger or to cheat the customer. The inevitable small amounts of sediment still remaining in a wine settle around the outside edge of this push-up and are not dislodged until almost the last drop of wine is poured. The flat-bottomed bottle, much cheaper to make, does not act this way, and the sediment begins to drift across this flat surface when the bottle is about three-quarters empty, with the result that the last glass or two will be cloudy. Filtering the wine before bottling will eliminate this problem, but the fact remains that Americans will accept a certain amount of sediment in a French wine, and none whatsoever in an American wine. This forces all of us to filter our wines more than we would like to, for there is no question that too heavy filtration can affect the taste of the wine. It would be nice if more people knew this and stopped returning bottles that contain even the faintest deposit. The French tend to regard a wine of some age with suspicion if it does not contain at least some sediment.

Another problem that 1956 brought to our attention was the question of vintage years. Nineteen fifty-six probably still stands as one of the worst years of the century in Europe, and one of the best in eastern America. Yet had we put 1956 on the neck label, the wine buffs would have looked at the charts of European vintage years and seen it put down as worthless. Even though the 1956 was the best we were to make for several years, we could have sold almost none with that fateful year on the label. It all goes back to that terrible "imported"-"domestic" syndrome. We like to think of our wine not as domestic but American. All others are foreign.

Anyway, the turbulent 1956 vintage was finally completed, punctuated by near disaster. Despite my best efforts, one of the seven-hundred-gallon casks heated to such a degree that the wax seal around the manhole by which the casks are entered and cleaned melted and the fermenting white wine began to spurt out in jets all over the concrete floor. All efforts to stop the leak were futile but by hurriedly pumping the wine off into any container that could be pressed into service the bulk of it was saved.

5

At about this time Sam Aaron, co-owner of what was at that time Sherry Wine & Spirits Company and today is Sherry-Lehmann, brought to our attention the fact that a lucrative competition was being sponsored by a liquor trade journal. It was an essay contest about some of the more uplifting aspects of the booze business. As I had been a writer, Sam suggested that I enter, and a few days later sent me the entry blanks. He also told me that the entries were read first by anyone who could be pressed into service, and that the surviving dozen or so were then read by professionals from Associated Press. He impressed on me the importance of being in that last group, and said that anything, badly written or not, which was expensively presented was almost guaranteed entry into this magic circle. So when I had finished my essay, which was entitled "Building a Regional Wine Business," I spent seventy-five dollars on the presentation: copious photographs, the essay done in Varityper, and a tooled leather binder with gold lettering.

Nothing happened for a long time after I submitted it, and just as I had decided it was seventy-five dollars down the drain I got a telegram. I was a winner, and the prize was two round-trip tickets to Paris. Paris was the last thing in both our minds at that particular moment, but the pull was irresistible. If we were to go at all we had to go right then, before the heavy summer work began. So notifying our customers that the winery would be closed for a month, we boarded a plane of Sabena Airlines. We were supposed to fly on a DC-7, but at the last moment we were supplied with a DC-6B, which meant that we had to land at Gander and again at Manchester, England, for refueling. Most of the trip was made in heavy fog and slashing rain and after coming into Manchester in fog so dense you couldn't see the wingtips we were relieved at the chance to have some tea. Of course the tea was good, but what made it memorable was the service, which I consider a perfect example of the paradox of Her Majesty's island. For it was served by a large motherly type in a flowered dress with sagging hems and bedroom slippers, and a tiny man completely gotten up in white tie and tails, with dirty fingernails.

Something like twenty hours after leaving New York we arrived in Brussels, and the remaining miles to Paris were made by helicopter. That part was enormously enjoyable, flying low over the fields, with the farmworkers looking up and waving. We landed in a *place* in downtown Paris, had our luggage cleared most informally in a wooden shed set up for the purpose, entered a taxi and were at our hotel in under fifteen minutes. A hasty supper and to bed, where we slept until late the next morning. We had arranged to get a car in one of the purchase/buy-back deals, Europe By Car, and to my total amazement it worked like a charm. The car was waiting for us in the morning, and when it was returned a month later they looked at it, said it was in A-1 condition, gave us our deposit back, and that was the end of it.

Because we were in a sense representing the American wine industry we had been liberally supplied with letters of introduction, and our first stop was with Alexis Lichine at Château

Lascombe on the Médoc peninsula. A gracious host and most knowledgeable man, Mr. Lichine made our three-day stay an event to be remembered. He arranged for us to visit all the top châteaus of the district, and supplied an English-speaking guide, Philip Togni, for all the visits. When we left him our trip was planned in advance, and letters were sent to various winemakers to expect us on such and such a day. Of course this made the schedule a little rigid, but it was more than made up for by the knowledge that we were expected, and that in Germany we had an English-speaking wine shipper at our disposal for two full days to cover the Rheingau district.

There were a few days' leeway in the itinerary, and we made the most of them. We had always wanted to have a meal at the Pyramide restaurant, and we managed to work it in. We had gone first to spend the night at the small hotel and restaurant at Roanne run by the Troisgros family, which, by the way, now has three stars although at the time it had two. When they heard we were winemakers the entire family converged on our table, and we produced a small bottle of our wine which we had brought along. They drank it solemnly and pronounced it good, although how much was courtesy is hard to say. Then they dispatched a son to the cellar for a bottle of Champagne, and then another. Finally, after dessert, cheese and coffee, someone remarked that we had not had the house's specialty, frogs' legs. Nothing would do but we had to have some, so we smilingly ate it at the end of a huge meal. The Champagne helped considerably. Everyone sat at our table and we were shortly joined by a local gynecologist, whose English was as voluble and as faulty as my French, all of which added a whole new dimension to the conversation. Finally, at midnight, full of cognac and various liqueurs, we staggered to bed, where I remembered that I had not got any bottled water. I went downstairs to buy a demi-Perrier, whereupon my host insisted that I drink a beer with him before retiring.

M. Troisgros had phoned ahead to make a reservation for lunch the next day at the Pyramide, but Alma's stomach was rebelling from the excesses of the previous evening. By the time we got to Vienne she was thoroughly sick, but she was determined to go through with it. We went in, she smiled, ate all of the superb meal, complimented the smiling and totally unaware Madame Point, got in the car, and a mile up the road lost it. A trouper through and through. We checked in for two nights at an inn a few miles farther along named Le Chapon Fin, which had a fine restaurant in its own right, but by now my friend was past caring. I went alone the next day to visit the Beaujolais proprietor who was expecting us, and who laid out an extensive lunch that Alma fortunately missed. In addition to his regular wine this gentleman made a rosé, a wine normally produced by crushing the red grape and allowing it to ferment for a day or so to extract only a part of the color from the skins before pressing and then allowing the fermentation to continue white-wine fashion. I asked him how he made his, and he candidly said that all the grapes not good enough for his regular wine, or which had begun to spoil, he immediately pressed and allowed to ferment like white. When I expressed amazement that the Gamay grape could develop so much color by this treatment, he gave me a generous dig in the ribs. "One can always add a barrel or two of red," he said, which makes one stop and think about the general quality of most rosés.

After resting at Le Chapon Fin we went on to Pouilly-Fuissé, a region whose white wine I have often thought resembled our own. Certainly the methods of vinification are identical, the soil is very similar, and although the grape is different I do not believe, as I said earlier, that this is as important as many people believe. Then on to Beaune and the marvelous Louis Latour establishment, run today by the grandson, Louis Noël Latour. They own the largest part of the slope at Corton Charlemagne, which I have always felt produces the finest white Burgundy, if not the finest dry white wine in the world. Many would disagree with this, but *"De gustibus . . ."* We were shown through the beautiful vineyards and immaculate winery, which Mr. Latour told us his grandfather had acquired for a song during the phylloxera epidemic, when everyone thought grapes could never be grown there again. We saw an amazing process, by which the cork of each bottle of white wine was drawn prior to shipping, the bottle held over a strong light, and a long hollow silver needle inserted to the bottom and run slowly and carefully around the crease at the edge of the push-up, where it sucks up minute deposits of sediment without decanting the bottle. This was done only for wine destined for America, and it was galling to think that anyone who would object to sediment in a Corton Charlemagne undoubtedly wouldn't appreciate the wine anyhow.

We had lunch with the Latour family, and afterward Mr. Latour approached us in some embarrassment. He speaks excellent English, but it is formal and does not extend to the idiomatic, particularly the American idiomatic. And it seemed that someone had given them a subscription to *The New Yorker,* but try as they might they could not make head or tail of the cartoons. I have seldom had a more enjoyable time than I had going over each picture, with its caption, explaining the background and the relevance each one had at a particular time. Slowly his face would light up, and he would hurriedly translate for his wife, who speaks little English, and then she would break into laughter. It was a marvelous session.

We had a day to spend before we were due in Wiesbaden, and we went again to the Black Forest, always one of our favorite spots. Checking into the same hotel we had stayed at five years earlier in Titisee, I chanced to mention this to the clerk. He flipped a couple of pages, looked up and said, "Efferett Crossby, from Vest Nyack." Looking at us sternly he said, "Und vere iss your daughter?"

(Another example of German efficiency occurred to us a few days later. We were driving a Renault Dauphine, a fine little car, but slightly ill at ease in Germany. In Mainz the hostility got too much and it simply quit cold in the middle of an intersection. I pushed it to the corner, while people watched with expressions that plainly said I was getting no more than I deserved by driving a French car. A gas station was nearby, and by a series of gestures, while pointing to the car and saying, *"Kaput,"* I managed to attract one of the men. He approached it gingerly, almost as though he were afraid he would catch something if he touched it. Having no idea what was wrong, he decided we needed gas, even though the gauge showed we had some, and he said it in a phrase that has always stood as the epitome of mad Teutonic construction. What he said was *"Nur ist Benzin alle,"* translatable as "Only is gasoline all." He put some in, the car coughed and decided to give it another try, and we went five or six blocks, when it became apparent that *"Nur ist Benzin alle"* was not the answer. This time we were near a garage, and repeating my dumb show I got the attention of a mechanic. He looked thoughtfully at the Dauphine, checked through his socket wrenches, picked out a certain size and marched up to the car. Lifting the engine cover, he shook the carburetor and said, "Ah." Apparently that model Dauphine had a tendency to have the carburetor come loose from the manifold, and this man knew it and just what size wrench to bring. A couple of quick turns, a modest payment, and we were on our way, not to be troubled again for the rest of the trip.)

Having checked into our hotel in Wiesbaden, we were met by the guide arranged for by Alexis Lichine. The young man, who spoke impeccable English, was to be at our disposal for the next two days, and we took full advantage of it. First we went to see the operation of Franz Karl Schmidt, a winegrower and wine shipper, where we watched the incredibly complicated process known as sterile bottling. Until the recent introduction of

97

some new fermentation retarders, which I never believed were sufficiently tested for me to use, there were only three ways to keep a wine from coming to life in the bottle: the addition of sulfur dioxide, the oldest method and the one we used; sterile filtration; and hot bottling, in which the wine is heated to the pasteurization point and put into hot bottles like so much tomato juice.

There was some years ago an interesting evaluation of these three methods in a trade magazine by the chief winemaker of one of the large California wineries. This gentleman said that sulfur dioxide, unless used very carefully, could be detected in the finished wine, which is true. Sterile filtration, he said, left the wine particularly vulnerable, so that the slightest contamination could ruin it, which is also true. Therefore, he concluded, hot bottling was the best method, "Although it does tend to have a deleterious effect on the flavor of the varietals." "Varietals" means quality wine in California, so what he was saying in effect was that it was still the best method, although it did make quality wine taste lousy.

Sterile bottling as we saw it in Wiesbaden consists of pumping the wine through such a fine filter medium that all the yeast cells and all stray bacteria are filtered out, leaving literally nothing in it that could bring the wine to life again in the bottle. This means that the bottles and the corks have to be at least as sterile, and the corks were soaking in a strong sulfur dioxide solution while the bottles were rinsed upside down on something resembling a drinking fountain that also sprayed their insides with liquid sulfur dioxide. This whole operation was carried on in a sealed and air-conditioned room by men wearing sterilized rubber gloves and masks. The bottles entered the room on a conveyor belt with rubber flaps that swung shut between bottles, were taken off and rinsed, put back on the belt, which took them through the filling and corking machine, and on to the outside through another set of flaps. As German wine

98

in all but the best years tends to be low in alcohol and is thereby doubly susceptible to spoilage, the operation we were watching allowed simply no room for error.

We also saw the steep hills of Nierstein, where the soil that washed down the hill during the year used to be laboriously carried up in wicker baskets on the backs of men. Now it's done by bucket loader and truck, but it is still one hell of a job, a job made necessary by the enormous value of the land and the impossibility of ever replacing any that is washed away for good.

We also attended a wine auction at the German State Wine Cellars at Eltville. The wine being tasted was that made the previous fall, 1956, which as mentioned earlier proved to be one of the poorest vintages of the century. In such years Germany permits the addition of both sugar and water, as does New York. France permits only the addition of sugar, and California only water. The reason for any of these additions is that in a poor year in a cold climate insufficient sugar develops in the grape, and it is the sugar that is converted into alcohol through the action of the yeast, which, to put it in the simplest of terms, eats the sugar and gives off two by-products: alcohol and carbon dioxide. Actually the process is more complicated than that, but it gives one the basic picture. The sugar is converted into alcohol at the basic rate of 50 percent of what the original sugar content was, and although this is also a rule of thumb and not entirely accurate it will suffice for now. In other words, if one starts with a grape containing 22 percent of sugar in its juice one should wind up with a wine containing 11 percent alcohol. Actually a well-made commercial wine will contain more than 11 percent from such a juice. But supposing the juice only contains 16 percent sugar? Then the wine will be about 8 percent alcohol, and such a wine will not be sound and will not keep. Also, there is a natural balance between the tartaric acid content and the sugar content of the grape. The

higher the sugar goes, the lower will be the acid, and vice versa.
So with a juice of only 16 percent sugar the acidity will be so
high as to render the wine practically undrinkable, and hence
the addition of water to lower the acidity and sugar to raise the
alcohol. New York State and Germany are cold, and frequently
have this problem. In New York up to 35 percent of a sugar-
water solution may be added to the juice in a bad year, and in
Germany 25 percent. French grapes, particularly in Burgundy,
are frequently low in sugar, but the resulting wines do not
suffer so much in quality when the acid is high. So the French
permit only sugar. California, due to its relentless sunshine,
runs too high in sugar, and water is permitted to reduce this.
The last thing they need there is extra sugar, so they virtuously
ban it. As one can see, each winegrowing district makes a virtue
of necessity.

Until recently no German wine that had sugar added could be
labeled *Originalabfüllung, Kellerabfüllung,* or *Kellerabzug.*
These phrases are equivalent to the French "Château Bottled,"
and mean that they were bottled by the man who grew the
grapes and produced the wine. But in France "Château Bottled"
or "Estate Bottled" wines could have sugar added, and this fact
was strongly resented by German winemakers. To make their
quality wines competitive with the French, this situation has
now been remedied, and beginning in 1971 all German wines
will fall into three categories:

The lowest will be *Tafelwein,* and like most ordinary table
wine it will probably be largely consumed in its country of
origin. The next is *Qualitätswein,* meaning a wine that has been
tasted and approved by a committee of growers from the district
of origin. It will carry an identifying number so that complaints
can be traced back to the source. This wine can be labeled
"Estate Bottled," and can be made with or without the use of
sugar. This group of wines will probably be that most widely
shipped to America.

At the top of the list is *Qualitätswein mit Prädikat,* which must be made without added sugar and which must start with a juice containing enough natural sugar to produce a wine of at least 10 percent alcohol. This wine will be entitled to the use of many of the old qualifying German phrases, and will be the only wine allowed to do so. Starting at the bottom of this exclusive group will be *Kabinett,* once a haughty if inconclusive designation, but now meaning the lightest and driest of the wines allowed into the sanctified group. Then will come *Spätlese* (picked later than normal ripening time), *Auslese* (specially ripe bunches picked while the remainder stays on the vine), *Beerenauslese* (overripe grapes picked berry by berry) and *Trockenbeerenauslese* (grapes which have been attacked by a special mold, and which have been picked one by one). This mold (*Botrytis cinerea*) saps the water from the grape and leaves no more than a drop of nectar in each one. It is called *Edelfaule* in Germany and *Pourriture Noble*—noble rot—in France. It is not a regular occurrence, but when it does happen it causes wine of remarkable sweetness and bouquet. I recall a small bottle of *Trockenbeerenauslese* being opened for us in a German winery, and the room was instantly filled with the scent of flowers. These wines are enormously expensive, and because of the sweetness and bouquet—as well as the price—are only for the most limited use.

But in 1957 the rules limiting the use of sugar were followed strictly, and at the wine auction we attended most of the wines were unsugared and were poor beyond belief. When buying critically, wine merchants never swallow the wine, as only a few swallows can blunt the fine edge of taste. It is swished around in the mouth, chewed on, breathed out through the nose, and spit out into a handy container. This is not chichi by any means, for with a little practice of sniffing and swishing and gurgling it is amazing how the wines begin to differentiate themselves even to the most neophytic palate. But at this particular auction, perhaps because the wines were so poor, people were not fussy where they spit them out, and the man sitting beside my wife consistently ejected his onto her right foot. Whether this was intended as a commentary on the wine or on Americans in general is hard to say.

In the afternoon we went to visit the small but very fine winery operated by Graf Jacob von Eltz, who in addition to the winery owns the family castle on the Mosel, Burg Eltz. It has been nationalized, but to keep partial ownership he and his wife have to live in it for a month or so each year. This was quite a chore, for it is drafty and uncomfortable, and the plumbing is rudimentary in the extreme. Also, no changes could be made without the approval of a committee of architects, and when he put up a small toolshed he was required to take it down at once, and then to apply for permission. The permission was granted, at which point he put the same shed up again. I rather like that. Too many times in this country a person is given permission to build a four-story building, puts up six, and then says, "But I didn't understand. Surely you're not going to make me take those two stories off? Think of the cost." Ninety percent of the time he gets away with it.

At this winery I saw again the massive use of plastic-lined steel tanks. I had seen them the day before at Schloss Johannisberg when we were taken behind what they themselves called their "iron curtain." There were rows and rows of them, which prompted me to ask what they were doing with the beautiful carved oak casks filling the great room at the front. Alas, they were window dressing, something with which to impress the tourists. And I must say that the plastic-lined tanks, pedestrian as they may be in appearance, simply have it all over the oak casks when it comes right down to winemaking qualities. They are easily cleaned, and there is no loss by evaporation through the pores as there is with wood. Further, wood dries out when not in use, and must be caulked and filled with water to swell it tight again before use, sometimes for a week or more. In addition, molds and spoilage bacteria get into the cracks and are extremely hard to remove. All of this would be worth the effort if the resulting wine were better, but it isn't. There is an exchange of wine and air through the staves of wood, and this exchange leads to oxidation. The last thing one wants in a fresh, clean white wine is oxidation, which darkens the color and thickens the taste. Oxidation is essential in most red wines, because aging is nothing more or less than controlled oxidation. But it can be ruinous for white wine. Also, as wine generates heat when fermenting, there is very little transfer of heat through a thick piece of oak. About the only way to cool wine fermenting in wood is to run it through a heat exchanger, and this is not a particularly good practice with quality wine. With a plastic-lined steel tank a simple garden sprinkler can be set on top, and cold water allowed to trickle down the sides. The wine can be kept as cool as desired through this simple method.

At the Jacob von Eltz winery I noticed a superb small crusher-stemmer, the best I had ever seen. The ones made in America were all too big for an operation of our size, and the small European ones I had seen before crushed the grapes before removing the stems. This one not only removed the stems first, but also removed any unripe berries before allowing the ripe ones to pass between the crushing rollers. And these, by the way, were soft rubber instead of metal or wood, and therefore could not crush the seeds and deposit excess tannin in the juice. I asked the Graf where he got such a machine. He said it was an Amos, and a friend of his in Mainz sold it. He drove me there and I bought one on the spot, writing out a check on my New York bank. It is a purchase I never regretted, and I never saw another like it in America. I also bought two plastic-lined steel tanks as soon as I returned home and these too proved highly satisfactory.

Our next stop was Ricquewihr in Alsace, at the winery and

vineyards of Jean Hugel. He was expecting us and was most cordial and helpful. He also had planned his sons well, for one was big and rustic, only interested in working in the vineyards; the other was frail and studious, only concerned with making the wine and looking after the business side of the venture. It seemed like too good a situation to last, and somebody told me in later years that it didn't. However, this may be only hearsay.

Alsace is the only French wine district to follow the California system of identifying the wine by naming it after the principal grape that goes into it. It is best known for a varietal named Gewürztraminer, a wine of exceptional bouquet. But this perfumy scent very quickly becomes overpowering, and after a glass or two one can drink no more. At least I can't. The Alsatians themselves rightly consider their Riesling to be their best wine. They also make a very pleasant, rather tart little wine out of the Sylvaner, sometimes called the Franken Riesling, although it is not a true Riesling at all.

Then finally on to the last stop—Champagne. We had been expected at Moët et Chandon, and were shown around by a majestic and courtly man known simply as Uncle Louis. His sole function seemed to be escorting visiting wine people, and we were lucky indeed to be numbered in that category. And what an operation he showed us. Champagne begins where most wines stop. It is a manufactured wine and begins with a regular and completely fermented white wine. For some reason Champagne tastes best when made from a rather thin, acid wine, and the still wines of Champagne are so acid that many people find them distasteful, although I rather like them on certain occasions.

Moët et Chandon, as do all the other top Champagne firms, has miles and miles of tunnels, cut deep in the soft rock. I was told that there were enough deep tunnels around Rheims, Épernay and Ay to protect the entire population of the area from bombings during World War II. And these tunnels contained endless stacks of finished and bottled white wine waiting to be transformed into Champagne.

When that magic moment comes the wine receives a carefully measured amount of sugar and live yeast so that a second fermentation will start in the bottle. But this time the carbon dioxide cannot escape and remains in the bottle in the form of bubbles. As in any fermentation, dead yeast cells fall to the bottom in the form of sediment, and getting rid of this sediment is the costliest part in the Champagne-making process. The bottle is put in a rack, pointing down but slightly tilted. Then, every day, men give the bottle a shaking twist, so that it slowly rotates. The shake loosens the sediment that tends to stick to the sides and causes it to drift downward into the neck. And the turn ensures that a different side of the neck will be up on different days, so that finally the bottle will be facing straight down, and all of the sediment will be resting securely and firmly packed on top of the inside of the cork. This process, by the way, is known as riddling.

The cork during this part of the Champagne's life is a temporary one, and is held in place by an *agrafe*, or clasp, which hooks under the lip around the Champagne bottle's neck. Now comes the ticklish business of getting the sediment out and keeping the Champagne in, a process known as disgorging. In the early days a man held the bottle upside down, popped out the cork letting the sediment and a goodly amount of wine spill out, stuck his thumb over the opening, turned it right side up, replaced the spilled Champagne with that from a spare bottle, recorked it with a permanent cork, held the cork in place with a wire hood, and that was that. Simple and enormously wasteful. The French poetically called this method "In full flight."

Yankee ingenuity came to the rescue, and one of the New York State producers of sparkling wines—believed to have been Great Western—began putting the neck of the bottle in freezing brine before popping the cork. This caused the sediment to freeze to the cork, so that the bottle could then be returned to the right-side-up position and the cork drawn in the normal manner, all of the sediment clinging neatly to it and almost no sparkling wine escaping. This process was quickly adopted by the French, and for many years it was the standard method of clearing sediment for Champagne. It was still tricky work, though, for Champagne builds up pressures of over one hundred pounds per square inch in the bottle, and many a bottle blew up in the face of a man carrying out this process, maiming or even blinding him. Heavy gauntlet gloves were used and a thick glass shield that separated the bottle from the worker, but accidents and much loss of Champagne still continued. Then a new method was developed, I believe in Germany, that spread quickly to the larger producers of sparkling wine in America, and finally to France.

This is the bottle transfer system, sometimes called the star system because it employs a huge pointed wheel, like a star with many points. The cork is pulled on a bottle of sparkling wine and the bottle is put firmly on one of these points under great pressure. The liquid is drawn out and pumped through a high-pressure filter, finally winding up in a clean bottle at another point in the "star." The first bottle is removed, quickly rinsed and put back on the star to receive the sparkling wine from another bottle, and this operation goes on and on. I have not recently seen a French Champagne plant in operation so I cannot comment on their current procedures. But I have watched some of the best American producers of sparkling wine over the last few years, and this is a fantastically efficient operation. In fact, the temporary cork referred to above is no longer used, and the new bottle is designed to take a beer cap. This stays on all during the second fermentation and is removed before the bottle goes onto the star by a device similar to what one sees on the front of Coke dispensers. There is no riddling, no disgorging and almost no waste.

Of course this involves the use of an extremely expensive machine, causing the small producers to stick to the old method. They even make a virtue of it, and perhaps justly. For though the new method fulfills the requirements of the law as far as the phrase "Naturally fermented in the bottle" goes, there can be no denying that it winds up in another bottle than the one in which it was fermented. So the people who stick to the older method have devised a new phrase—"Naturally fermented in *this* bottle." They may have a point, but one must take into consideration the fact that while a great deal of the world's fine still wines comes from the smallest producers, this is not true of Champagnes and other sparkling wines, which are manufactured wines. In producing these the bigger companies have the edge in equipment and technology, and generally turn out a better product. By this I mean those large producers who *try* to turn out a quality product, not those enormous factories that make oceans of "champagne" in huge stainless steel pressure tanks out of table grapes, and bottle it like so much Dr Pepper.

We ended our visit at Moët et Chandon with Uncle Louis opening a bottle of Dom Pérignon, their finest-quality product, which they make in small amounts. The real Dom Pérignon was an ecclesiastic who is often credited with discovering Champagne. Today, though, it is generally believed that he was the first to use a cork for a closure, and thus keep the bubbles in the wine. Sparkling wine was known long before the time of Dom Pérignon, but the available closures, twine soaked in olive oil, for instance, were inefficient and unreliable, and not until the introduction of cork was it possible to keep them for any length of time.

Before leaving the subject of Champagne let me say a few words about "brut," "extra dry," "demisec," etc. Sugar is a great masker of poor quality. The reason that the kosher type wines, made from Concord grapes, are sweet has nothing to do with the natural sweetness of the grape. Actually there is very little sugar in Concords, and a wine made without artificial sweetening would be undrinkable. For my palate it is undrinkable even when sweetened, and a dry Concord wine is absolutely ghastly. "Dry," of course, is the term used to describe a wine in which all the sugar has been converted to alcohol, and there is no discernible natural sweetness left. Any fault in a bone-dry wine stands out like the proverbial sore thumb, and these faults are masked by adding sugar, which deadens the palate by overpowering the taste. This explains why "brut" Champagne, the driest of them all, is always the most expensive. It is made from only that Champagne that can measure up to the taste test of absolute dryness, which of course means the best. All the rest go through a process called "dosage," where, depending on the quality, varying amounts of sugar syrup are added at the final corking. "Brut," therefore, is the driest, followed by "extra dry," which strange to say is not as dry. They are followed in order by "sec," "demisec," and "doux," which is downright sweet. There are other classifications, such as "English Market," but the above list is what one generally encounters in this country. I should add that American "Champagne" makers have been known to label a bottle of "demisec" as "brut," on the theory that Americans know it is chic to order "brut" but don't really like it that dry. No comment.

Not having been too entranced with our twenty-four-hour transatlantic flight, we discovered in Paris that we could turn in our return airplane ticket, and by paying a modest extra sum switch our reservations to the *Liberté*. We had made the same trip on this ship in 1937, when it was the *Europa*, and by an incredible coincidence wound up in exactly the same cabin we had had twenty years earlier. We were saddened when it was scrapped a few years later, as we have been saddened at the disappearance one by one of so many of the great ships. We have loved the life aboard ships, great or small, and from 1963 until 1970 the Grace liner *Santa Rosa* became like a second home as we made trip after trip going to and coming from our home in Jamaica. What a pity, if not to say disgrace, that the National Maritime Union finally succeeded in pricing the American Merchant Marine out of the seas, and how tragic that a penny-pinching government failed to come to the rescue. How many people know that no passenger ship carrying the American flag is at sea today, with the exception of a few cruise ships on the West Coast? The *United States,* the *Independence,* the *Constitution,* the passenger ships of the Moore-McCormack lines, the Grace line, the Matson line, the American President Line—all gone from their regular runs.

6

We arrived back at High Tor the third of June, 1957, to find that almost nothing I had told the two juvenile delinquents left in charge had been done. This is not to say that they had been idle, for a good deal of time had been spent in seeing how fast they could spin the truck in the confined gravel strip in front of the winery, the final result being that it was driven full tilt into the side of the building, smashing a fender and a headlight, and knocking down the post holding the electric conduit. We fired one and kept the other. Apparently we made the right choice, for some years later I had the pleasure of receiving a letter from the one we kept, thanking me for what I had done for him and for getting him squared away in life.

Everyone turned to and finally a semblance of order was restored out of the near chaos we had found. The summer weather was good, the grapes grew well, and soon it was obvious that a good vintage was in the offing. Not as exuberant as 1956 as far as quantity went, but of fine quality.

In late August, shortly before the harvest was about to begin, we were informed that *Life* magazine was sending a reporter and a photographer to cover our annual Labor Day vintage party. By now it had swelled to more than two hundred guests, not all of whom were friends or even acquaintances. The fame of the party had spread, and people had begun to call and ask when the "festival" would be held. They seemed undeterred when told that it was by invitation only.

Sam Aaron called the day before the party to say that Alexis Lichine was in town and would like to come out. We were naturally very pleased at this and he arrived just as the early guests were picking up their baskets to go into the vineyards to gather a ritual bushel of grapes each. We had learned from the year before: limiting each participating guest to one bushel, we would not be inundated. The *Life* people had not yet arrived, so I took Sam and Alexis into the back of the winery to taste some of our products.

We started with the white, the '53, '54, '55 and '56 being by now in bottle. All were approved, some more so than others, and then we started on the red. The '56 was still in cask, but the '53, '54 and '55 were in bottle, the latter for only a few weeks. The first two of these were solid, rather heavy and deeply colored wines, and Lichine gave them a good rating. But a visiting French winemaker had stopped by the year before and had ventured the opinion that perhaps they were a shade too heavy. He suggested that I add a touch of white wine to give them a little more "finesse." Being short on 1955 red, and also being overly impressed with French winemakers in general rather than in particular—for the particular French winemaker is perhaps the world's best while the general is often run of the mill—I gave it a try (the unfortunate decision referred to earlier) and the '55 we were about to sample contained a generous addition of white wine. Lichine took a sip, rolled it around in his mouth, chewed on it for a while, spit it out on the floor and tried again. Finally he uttered the words that still stand as my favorite personal wine quote.

"Everett," he said, "I think that perhaps this wine is aiming for a finesse it does not inherently possess."

This sounds like the sort of chichi that I will discuss later when I get going on the "wine critics." But it was in fact eminently correct, and eminently sound. Our red wines have always been essentially solid and they should never be lightened. The phrasing sounded hokey simply because of the courtly way in which Alexis Lichine always uses the English language.

Just at that moment one of the uninvited guests, a short man in bermudas and bobbysocks, wandered into the back room and there we were, sniffing, snortling, chewing, going through all the routine maneuvers that make wine tasting resemble an intricate courting dance conducted by a strange, tall species of featherless birds. He looked at us in shocked wonder, and when we got to the part where the wine was spit out on the floor he turned and shouted, "Ethel, come back here. You'll never believe what they're doing."

The *Life* group finally arrived. It consisted of an extremely attractive young woman reporter who seemed hesitant about throwing her weight around (what there was of it), an editor and a very active young photographer. He and the editor listened gloomily while we told them how the party was conducted, and then they shook their heads. Not enough action. Never be accepted. Got to jazz it up.

First they decided we should have a contest to see which woman guest had the biggest feet, the winner to be allowed to tromp out some grapes in a small washtub. I hasten to add that these grapes were thrown out afterward. That didn't sound like such a bad idea, nor did fixing it so that a statuesque brunette who looked as if she had been born to spend her life in wine vats would win. The place was alive with celebrities, our friends and neighbors, and writer John Masters, comic-strip artist Milton Caniff and cartoonist Bill Mauldin were chosen as judges and told whom to vote for. Through it all the young photographer danced around like a whirling dervish, but the contest was fun and everyone enjoyed it.

Next it was decided that there should be some sort of ceremony about bringing the grapes down from the vineyards, and a dozen or so of the tallest men were chosen to march solemnly past, each hefting a brimful bushel basket of grapes on one shoulder. By now the interest of the guests was beginning to wane, and so for a time at least I was able to bridle the energy of the rampant young photographer. But he had heard that Alexis Lichine was present, and seeing an important-looking person sporting a beard and wearing a beret, he decided that he was the one. When the pictures were developed a good quarter of them were of a rival photographer named Barrett Gallagher, who also did much of his work for the *Time-Life-Fortune* chain.

As evening drew on there was general agreement by the *Life* contingent that more action was needed. A serpentine dance was arranged around the barrels and casks inside the winery, with Burgess Meredith pretending to conduct Turk Murphy, who in turn pretended to be playing a tune on the spout of a copper wine-pouring can. Our guests were good sports, for they knew this was all designed to help us, but soon I could see them beginning to wilt. I called a halt, vetoing the possibility of a torchlight parade, and the photographer sadly packed his equipment and went home.

In a few days a friend at *Life* told me that the story had been rejected. Can you guess why? Officially the reason given was that the presence of so many celebrities made it perfectly apparent that the whole thing was a put-up job, no such party was in fact a regular fixture. I should point out that with the exceptions of Alexis Lichine and Turk Murphy, all the others— Burgess Meredith (who brought Murphy), John Masters, Milton Caniff, Bill Mauldin, Henry Varnum Poor, cartoonist Dave Breger, Mitch Miller—were our near neighbors and friends who had been to the preceding parties and continued to come until the parties were discontinued a few years later.

I could not escape the suspicion that another reason the story was not accepted was the frenetic pace at which it had been shot, and the transparent artificiality of it all. People were conned into doing things they would not normally have done, and it showed. I am not blaming the *Life* people, who were simply trying to do a job on what may perhaps have been by their standards an impossible assignment. But the whole thing about the party, the thing that made it memorable year after year in the minds of the participants, was its basic simplicity—a group of people who knew each other, liked each other, and who most of all were helping two friends celebrate the arrival of another vintage. I think the simplicity and authenticity would have shone through if the guests had been allowed to do their thing, celebrities chatting over a glass of wine with gas station owners, plumbers and professors.

It was a great blow. The winery was bursting with produce of the previous bumper year, and a story in *Life* would have put us in a financial position to expand at a time when I was still young and full of energy. Nothing, however, works that way, and when the lightning finally struck in early 1971 I had already made the decision to either sell or phase out the operation. With this in mind I had deliberately and methodically been reducing the inventory so that I would not be in the position of having to sell wine at a fire-sale price of ten cents on the dollar. Today, as a result of all the newspaper, magazine and book articles about us, I could sell ten times what I have on hand. As a former English employee used to say, "Makes you think, doesn't it?"

One more misadventure befell us that year of 1957. A week or so after the unsung party a hurricane was reported to be nosing its destructive way up the East Coast. About half the crop was still on the vine, and we worked from early morning until after dark to get in as many grapes as possible before it hit. But we had friends, Gil and Mildred Burck, to whom we had been giving surplus grapevines for several years until by 1957 they had roughly three hundred of bearing age. Gilbert Burck, by the way, was a senior editor of *Fortune,* and is the father of Charles Burck, who wrote an excellent article on California wines which I will quote later.

By now the three hundred vines were producing far more grapes than they could convert into wine with their limited facilities, and we set up a system by which they brought the picked grapes to High Tor and we would crush and press them. They took back as much juice as they could handle, and the rest went into our own vintage. It was an excellent arrangement and a good deal for everyone.

But this year they somehow didn't hear of the hurricane or were otherwise preoccupied and did nothing about the crop until the morning the storm was due to hit. At the crack of dawn Gilbert, Mildred and Charles went out under the ominous skies and started to bring in the crop, frantically picking in the face of the rising wind, filling everything available—laundry baskets, washtubs, mop buckets, anything at all—with grapes. Finally it was done, and the grapes safely under cover. But Gil has many things on his mind and his immediate memory span is not of the longest. He forgot all about the hurricane. Without saying anything to the rest of the family, he packed the grapes into his Jaguar Mark VII and drove over to High Tor, arriving just as the storm was hitting its peak. He drove up to where I was cowering in the entrance to the winery and got out.

"Hi, Everett," he said. "I brought some grapes over."

"But, Gil," I said. "The hurricane."

"What hurricane?" he said dreamily, while trellis posts were falling like tenpins behind him.

To take my mind off the damage going on outside, I decided to press his grapes. The power, of course, was out, but I started up the generator, threw the special switch from "Line" to "Generator," and crushed and pressed his entire crop while the storm howled outside.

We suffered considerable damage, but the long-range effect was minimal. Some twenty end posts were blown down, and naturally the wires went over with them. This, of course, left the grapevines spread out all over the ground and it was a real chore to pick the bunches that were embedded in the sodden earth. But for the Burcks it was a year they will never forget, and to this day they always refer to the wine they made from that crop as the "Hurricane Vintage."

7

Two things happened after the 1957 vintage was in. One of my brothers and I were given our inheritance while our mother was still around to enjoy and appreciate what we did with it. The financial heat was now off. Second, rather reluctantly I entered the firing line of politics. By instinct I have always preferred to be behind the scenes, pulling levers, turning wheels. But a situation came about that almost forced me to step up front, and while the financial heat was off, the personal heat was now about five hundred degrees.

I am and have always been a Democrat. I became twenty-one on June tenth of 1932, and in that November I cast my first vote for FDR. But this is simply to set the stage. I have the most profound respect for anyone who takes a position, works for his party, whatever it may be, and stands by it. The extremes at both ends of the spectrum tend to be something of a drag, but I would never try to deny anyone his right to feel and vote the way he does. I am more at home in the company of a good Republican than a poor Democrat.

My party suffered a stunning defeat at the polls in Clarkstown in November of 1957. I was approached to take over the reins from the fumbling hands that held them, and without thinking too much about the consequences I agreed. In New York State, a great deal of power is wielded by an entity known as the "township," and though the township in which I lived was basically Republican we always managed to elect some qualified Democrats. There were ten elected offices in our town, normally split six–four, seven–five even eight–two in favor of the Republicans. But after the 1957 election the split was nine–one, the only Democratic winner being the lady receiver of taxes who had held the job for many years and who had taken over the job from her father, who had held it for years before her. In fact, a widely quoted saying at the time was that she could win running on a laundry ticket. The town council, the governing body of the town, was for the first time in its history five to nothing Republican.

I accepted the challenge, and I must have done something right, for two years later in the next township election I ran five candidates, none of whom had ever been elected to office before. Three were elected, and a fourth lost by only thirty-seven votes out of a total of almost eleven thousand. If this man had won we would have taken control of the town council, something we did four years later.

But as I said, this role was foreign to me. At the end of four years I stepped down, chalking it up as one more of the many careers that I have always seemed to be in the process of filling. For like so many performers and writers of today, I have had my share of jobs. It is popular for people in the arts to speak of being waiters, ditchdiggers, longshoremen and all the rest when they were young. Unlike most of them, my jobs did not tend toward the physical until the last and most challenging of them all—High Tor Vineyards. I started as a schoolteacher after graduation from the University of Southern California, going on to concert singing in and around New York City, as well as radio acting. In 1940 I took a job—for peanuts, I might add—

at the New York World's Fair. It was at the RCA exhibit demonstrating television to the American public for the first time. Ten or fifteen people would be herded into a small room to watch on an eight-by-ten-inch screen a closed-circuit showing of live performers doing their thing on a stage at the other side of the building. I was billed as "Television's Favorite Baritone," and I worked in the company of people such as Burr Tillstrom with his Kukla and Ollie (Fran came along later), Earl Wrightson, billed as that "The Grand Baritone," Burl Ives, and a vivacious and black-haired young lady named Dinah Shore. The first time Dinah tried out it was noticed that she had a wide gap between her upper front teeth, and before she went on camera I took a chunk of white wax and with thumb and forefinger plugged the gap. The gap is now gone, as is the dark hair. But she is still my favorite female vocalist.

The fair ended at the end of October 1940, and it was time to do some reckoning. I had decided that if I didn't make it as a singer by the time I was thirty I would chuck it, and on the following June I would be thirty. I had done some concertizing, sung on a few radio network shows, been in a tiny part in a Broadway show which ran two weeks, and only the year before had had a role in a perfectly dreadful musical that closed on the road, leaving us all stranded in Rumford, Maine.

A friend we had met in the disastrous musical, who felt about tap-dancing the way I was beginning to feel about singing, suggested that he and I try writing a play, which we did. And miraculous to say, this first effort came within one thin hairline of being produced. The man who was to put it on had raised all the money required, but unfortunately for us decided to get a little insurance money from a friend in Washington. This worthy not only put up no money but talked the producer out of doing the play at all. It was six years before we finally sold something.

In the meantime some sort of income was necessary, so without a backward glance at singing I turned to something I was already doing on a semiprofessional basis, photography. Alma and I set up a portrait studio in our penthouse on East Seventy-third Street, which already had a large and well-equipped darkroom, and for the next two years we made quite a bit of money, Alma concentrating on the more or less informal shots while I took the formal ones of the elderly fogies, using a five-by-seven-inch studio camera. During this time I found time to write and orchestrate a rather lengthy symphonic piece and invent an all-electronic color television system. Unfortunately, I did not have the formal training to carry my invention all the way through by myself, and I took the basic idea to Dr. Alfred Goldsmith, a pioneer in television and television systems. He agreed that the idea had merit, and took on the job of technical consultant. I drew up my ideas as best I could and he would put them into scientific terms, until at last it was complete. I applied for a patent in late 1941, and the application was promptly rejected. Dr. Goldsmith and my patent attorney, Carl Cohen, explained to me that this was an "office action," something the patent office always does with first submissions of neophyte inventors. They take a look at the subject matter and then run through the files on anything that even remotely resembles it. With all of this quoted as "prior art," the claim is perfunctorily turned down.

This seems to be what happened in this first rejection, for many of the previous patents quoted as "prior art" had almost nothing to do with my invention. But we revised it and tried again in early 1942, and after a considerably longer wait it was again rejected. This time someone had really studied it and only those systems that had had at least some similarity to mine were quoted.

I carefully went over all the papers again, for after a third rejection you have had it. My system did contain much that was not covered by any previous patent, and after concentrating on

The Concord grapevine on the terrace in New York City.

Alma, Averill, and the bare beginnings of the winery at High Tor, 1951.

Everett and a vine, also in 1951.

Everett, Alma, and Elmer Van Orden picking for the first commercial vintage in 1953.

Hand loading the grapes into the crusher.

Loading the electric press for the first commercial vintage.

Inside the winery, showing the crusher and the electric press in operation.

Aging the wine in wooden casks. *(Al Wegener)*

Hand corking the bottles.

Getting ready for
Craig Claiborne's
visit. *(Al Wegener)*

The first job of the year is pruning the vines.

A properly pruned vine.

The vineyard is cultivated in early spring.

The vines grow rapidly and are tied to the supporting trellis to let the tractor get through.

The vines must be sprayed six to eight times during the summer.

Tobacco netting protects the grapes from the birds.

On a fine, August day,
the picking of the ripe grapes
begins.

The picking continues through
September...

. . . not ending usually until a cold day in October.

The grapes are passed through the crusher.

The pulp goes into the vats for the primary fermentation.

After primary fermentation, the pulp (seeds, skin, and juice) is pumped into the press.

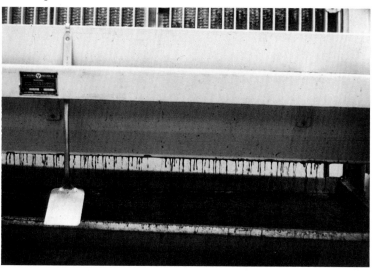

The raw wine collects in the pan from the press.

After aging, bottling,
and corking, the wine is
laid down in bins to acquire
bottle age.

After proper aging, the
wine is hand labeled.

The finished product—a Rockland White—light, dry, delicious.

that we crossed our fingers and filed for the last time. After weeks of waiting we were notified that while three of the claims were disallowed, the other fifteen were accepted, and a patent on them was granted. It need not have been, for nothing ever happened. All the networks were interested, but not to the extent of putting up money. A patent is good for seventeen years, and mine expired in 1959, before color television became a full reality. The networks knew that the patent was ahead of its time and simply allowed it to expire, when the ideas it contained were free for the use of anybody.

In the meantime, Pearl Harbor had happened, and photographic materials became harder and harder to come by. So when I was offered a job directing radio programs for the Office of War Information, which later became the Voice of America, I took it, while Alma continued the photographic business on a limited basis.

As I had a good working knowledge of Spanish, I was shortly made the executive producer of the Iberian section, in charge of the announcers, actors and newscasters working in Spanish and Portuguese. I knew no Portuguese at all, but in those hectic times it didn't matter. The job provided me with the archetype of the civil service syndrome that has plagued my years at High Tor.

We were broadcasting directly to Spain and Portugal, and we could not use Argentinians or Mexicans for Spain nor Brazilians for Portugal. There were quite a few articulate Spaniards around, and we had little trouble finding announcers who could lisp their way through the intricacies of the c's and z's, but Portuguese was something else again. After a diligent search we found two young men with sufficient education to pronounce the language properly, good enough voices, and the ability to read a newscast at sight. One will therefore imagine the delight of one and all when a man walked into our building looking for work, a man who not only spoke impeccable Portuguese but had for some time been a commentator on Portuguese radio. We hired him at once and sent in his papers for security clearance, using him in the meantime on a "purchase order," or temporary, basis.

Two weeks later I received a call from the local head of Civil Service, telling me to get rid of the man at once. Was he subversive? Was he perhaps at outs with the Portuguese government? None of these things. It was simply that he was not married to the lady he was living with, by whom he had three children. This seemed so outrageous that I made the mistake of laughing. It was no laughing matter. No United States funds could be spent on someone living in sin. In vain I pointed out that he was one of only three Portuguese announcers in all of New York, and that without him the entire Portuguese effort might have to be abandoned. It was agreed that such a possibility was most unfortunate, but was still not as bad as giving federal money to a man who had fathered three illegitimate children.

So we let him go, but when one of the other two announcers became seriously ill it was time for strong remedies. One of the program directors who worked in our section went with me to call on the announcer, who was sitting confused and unemployed in his apartment.

My friend looked at him and said, "Let's face it, João, you've got to get married."

"But why?" asked the puzzled man.

"Who knows? But you've got to."

I looked at the woman. "Do you have any objections to getting married?"

"No," she said. "I guess not. It just seems sort of—how to say—stupid."

"It is," we said in unison, "but do it."

They looked at each other and shrugged. Out they went to get a Wassermann and a license. It being wartime, the waiting period was suspended, so they marched to a municipal judge, who tied the knot while their three children looked on. I sent the certificate to the Civil Service man, who said to put him on the payroll immediately, for outside of that one fault he was as clean as a hound's tooth.

And so João went back to work, bewildered but a better man. And the United States government in all its majesty had made an honest woman out of a Portuguese lady who couldn't have cared less.

After the Voice of America I spent a year in the advertising jungles of Madison Avenue, producing a radio program appropriately entitled "It Pays to Be Ignorant." Then my partner and I sold our first radio script and we were off to the races, writing for a couple of years together, and then singly.

I have run through this catalogue to show the backward nature of my life, for as I said, most first authors start by doing menial work, and gradually work into the more cerebral. My varied early careers contained no physical effort whatsoever, and it wasn't until I was almost forty that High Tor Vineyards turned me into a combined stevedore, ditchdigger and baggage smasher. And this was the only job that has ever had sufficient challenge to make me want to stick with it. One can easily say that I gave up singing and acting because I didn't make a huge success of it, but I have seen many a sad creature following that golden bubble long after all hope of success had passed by. No, it simply didn't interest me all that much. An actor takes the thoughts and words of a writer and passes them through his head and out of his mouth. The more easily they pass through, the better the actor. A director maneuvers his body. An actor is essentially a vessel, and like all vessels, the hollower it is the more capacity it has. Actors make marvelous friends, charming conversationalists and interesting lovers. But they should never be elected governors.

The same thing goes for my political career. The failure of

political leaders can be laid to either stupidity, sloth or corruption. It is easy to clean the rotten apples out of the political barrel, put up some decent candidates and win, providing one never loses sight of that magical coefficient "feasibility." It is necessary to back an occasional lost cause, to run a candidate now and then who is intellectually qualified while at the same time is a born loser, if only to keep the opposition more or less honest. But one must never forget the feasible. Otherwise one will spend the rest of one's life running Adlai Stevensons, and electing nobody.

But wine is a challenge that never ends, because no two wines and no two seasons are ever alike. The leaves fall, the wood grows hard. The snow comes, and the naked vines stand out in the empty night, alone and unprotected. What will happen to them *this* year? What form will the pruning take in the early days of spring? Each vine must be examined and trimmed according to how well it grew the previous summer, and how well it survived the winter. Then the sap runs, the growth starts once again. No two springs proceed in the same way. Maybe it will be cold and wet, or maybe unduly warm, bringing unseasonal growth and the chance of being caught by a late frost. Will June be cool? How many sprays will we have to use to keep at bay the ever lurking bugs and blights that prey upon the vines? Will late summer be hot and dry, bringing the acid down and the sugar up to the peak of perfection? Or will it rain during the ripening period, forcing more liquid into the grape than the ripened skin can hold, causing it to burst and spill the juice on the berries below, which in turn will cause them to rot? Will the birds be kind or will they literally destroy the harvest? And what about the yellowjackets, which in their search for liquid, any liquid, punch holes in the grapes, reducing each bunch to a soggy mess?

Then it is over (generally before one is quite prepared) and the grapes are in and the winemaking has begun. In most other fruit-growing endeavors this is the end of the line, but with wine it is just the beginning. An apple is picked, an apple is shipped, an apple is eaten, period. But to the winemaker the crucial time is at hand. No two fermentations ever go exactly alike, and the young wine must be watched as an infant is watched. Will it turn moodily sick, or will it bound exuberantly upward into excellence? And even as the winemaker ponders these matters the leaves are falling, the wood is growing hard, the snow falls and the vines renew their never ending battle with the cold. The whole cycle is beginning again, and it is a challenge not only to the vines but also to the winemaker. One must be an optimist, I think, to be a successful vineyardist, and if I am nothing else I am that. The challenge must be confidently met as we met it for more than twenty years, and if one does not have complete faith in the ultimate outcome then the challenge is not worth facing. I have enjoyed this challenge and though unhorsed in many a joust I have ridden out each spring with the sure conviction that nothing can possibly go wrong this time.

It is this inevitability, this being at the beck and call of a gigantic force too complex to understand, that the neophyte winemaker finds so hard to fathom. There can be no long-range planning during the growing season for the simple reason that there can be no long-range planning of the weather. In the winter, with snow on the ground and the vines asleep, the work of bottling, labeling, racking, evaluating can proceed on a more or less preplanned schedule. But in the summer everything must hang loose. No fine, quiet, clear and cool day can be squandered on inside work, for this is a luxury that may cost the winemaker dearly. It makes no difference that he has made plans to bottle on Tuesday and Wednesday. If a spraying is coming up, and the vines need tying before the sprayer can run the rows, the bottling must wait if Tuesday dawns fair. The orders? The orders can wait. The grapes cannot.

Consider. Supposing you did your planned bottling on Tuesday. You are now committed to bottle again on Wednesday, for the half-empty cask left over from Tuesday cannot wait and must be bottled now. And if both days are fair the small labor force available that would have completed the tying on Tuesday so that you yourself could spray on Wednesday has been wasted on inside work. So the tying will be done on Thursday. But Thursday brings with it a cold windy drizzle. No outside work is possible, and the transient summer workers, paid by the hour, while away the time doing clean-up chores and repairs, none of them essential. Friday and Saturday are also wet, but Sunday is fine again. On Sunday, however, the local high school boys who constitute the transient help are not scheduled to work, and urgent calls reveal that they are all going to attend a rock festival, or whatever.

You, your wife, your one full-time man, who will ask for an extra day off in return for working Sunday, and one boy saving for a motorcycle who wants the money more than the rock, work all day and get perhaps two-thirds of the tying done. Monday the job is finished by noon, but by then the temperature is in the nineties, and grapes should not be sprayed at eighty-five or above. Tuesday is blistering, and even though you are on the sprayer at five in the morning the vineyards are no more than half sprayed before it is once more too hot.

Wednesday it rains, Thursday it rains and Friday the job is finished, over a week behind schedule. And because of the heat and the rain, the first telltale signs of downy mildew are already showing, and you know that part of the crop will be lost, just for squandering two days.

In 1957 we were young enough to assume that we would probably live forever, and the problems that concerned us were the problems of the moment, like the beacon that had flashed nightly from the top of High Tor, and was considered obsolete because of all the new electronic equipment that now guided planes ostensibly more safely to their destinations. One night it was lighting up the sky as usual, and the next it was dark. After stewing about it awhile we called Milton Caniff, who had several times mentioned that he drew solace in seeing it sweep past his window late at night while he was trying to get ideas for his comic strip "Steve Canyon." Milton told us what we had failed to read in the paper, that the Civil Aeronautics Administration was phasing it out and that it would soon be dismantled. However, if a sponsoring agency of enough respectability could be found that would guarantee its maintenance, the CAA would turn over the light and allow it to continue.

And so a plot was born. Milton has always stood very high with the Air Force, and particularly with the Civil Air Patrol, and it was decided that he would approach the CAP to be the sponsoring agency. Alma and I had two rather oddly assorted friends, the president of Orange and Rockland Utilities, our local light and power company, and the head of the International Brotherhood of Electrical Workers. If the CAP would agree to accept the sponsorship we would ask the light company to supply free electricity, and IBEW to supply free maintenance of the light and the cable running to it.

Everyone accepted, and in about a week a meeting was held at Caniff's that was attended by Colonel Morris of the CAP, Charles Hulswit, then president of the public utility company, and Pat Damiani of the electrical workers' union. All the details were worked out, and even the New York Trap Rock Corporation got into the act by agreeing to furnish the liability insurance. In the light of such a prestigious group the CAA had not much option, and they agreed to turn the light and all its accompanying equipment over to the CAP as soon as possible. The only unhappy party in on the deal was the Palisades Interstate Park Commission, on whose land the light was located. This group has always been allergic to anything on their property that they do not own and control, and they desperately wanted to tear the whole thing down. But we saw to it that it received so much publicity that even the commission's well-known arrogance was finally forced to bow to public demand.

A word at this point about the New York Trap Rock Corporation. In 1939 the town of Clarkstown passed its first zoning ordinance, an ordinance that placed certain lands purchased a few years earlier by Trap Rock for quarrying purposes in a newly created residential zone. A good many public meetings were held whereby any person or company who felt that his rights had been infringed could come and put his complaint on record. And although the stone-quarrying company had more at stake than anyone else affected by this ordinance, it never sent anyone to any of the meetings, simply disdaining to defend what it was sure could be successfully challenged at court when the time was ripe. And so the ordinance was passed.

In the early 1950s the need for quarrying this potentially enormously valuable land arrived, and they brought a rather cursory request before the town board asking permission to blast and quarry in what was by now a highly restricted zone. This request was unanimously denied, and the New York Trap Rock Corporation went to court. The action was heard before Judge Coyne, known to some of his associates as Reversible Coyne.

As Alma and I had a 1,200-foot common boundary with Trap Rock, we rode like twin Paul Reveres through the district to stir up opposition, a task that did not prove to be difficult. And when the case came to trial at the county courthouse in New City I endeared myself to the quarrying interests by testifying the better part of a morning about the adverse effects the blasting and the dust would have on the vineyards. It was following this testimony that a most incredible exchange took place between me and the presiding judge. As I was walking down the hall at the noon recess, Judge Coyne caught up with me.

"All those terrible things that might happen to the vineyards wouldn't really happen, would they?" he said.

I looked at him in blank amazement. "Your honor, I was testifying under oath."

He looked at me and laughed. "Oh, that," he said, and walked on.

It came as no surprise to anyone that he ruled in favor of the New York Trap Rock Corporation. It also came as no surprise that Judge Coyne lived up to his reputation by being promptly reversed by the Appellate Division. This reversal was upheld by the highest court in New York, the Court of Appeals, and when Trap Rock chose to take it to the last authority the reversal was once more upheld by the United States Supreme Court. One would have thought that would have been enough, but Martin Marietta has bought out the Trap Rock interests and now, almost twenty years later, is trying to reopen this can of worms.

But on that day in 1957 when the transfer was to take place all the sponsors gathered at our house, where a government official handed over title to the light to Colonel Morris. Then the Trap Rock company's helicopter ferried the guests to the summit for the relighting ceremonies, one at a time. As I was then such a thorn in the side of the quarry company, I decided they just might consider the helicopter expendable when it came time to get me, and I hiked up the mountain, carrying five bottles of wine and three dozen paper cups. I arrived at the top just as the helicopter settled down with its last passenger, at which point about a dozen CAP planes solemnly circled the mountain and returned to their field.

The light was lit, numerous toasts were drunk and the bottles symbolically smashed at the base of the tower. And then, in response to a secret call Caniff had made to Stewart Air Base, a few miles up the river, a whole wing of jet fighters came screaming down over the Hudson, passing us at an altitude no higher than the summit of our mountains. The whole corny spectacle gave the Crosbys and the Caniffs—hambones to the core—a glow they have never forgotten. In fact, when it was all over and all the guests had gone, Alma celebrated by breaking out in one of the worst rashes I have ever seen.

Almost immediately the mechanism that turned it on at night and off in the morning broke down, and until the union got another to take its place Alma and I turned it on and off by hand from a switch by our entrance gate. We did this for over a month and we took it very seriously. I remember once we had finished dinner in a restaurant about five miles away, and were settling down to some leisurely Cognac.

Suddenly Alma said, "My God, the light!"

We gulped the Cognac, explained the emergency to a somewhat bemused restaurateur and dashed home to switch on the light, about a half hour late. The phone was ringing. Caniff wanted to know if we were ill.

On another occasion Alma had attended a meeting in West Nyack and was returning home on a road that had the summit of High Tor dead ahead. Suddenly she realized the light was dark, that I was either sick or somehow incredibly had forgotten—which proved to be the case. And even as she looked the great beam sprang out to light up the night. She tells me she murmured to herself, "Good man."

During the years that we managed to keep it lit the IBEW did far more than they had bargained for. The light itself was a World War I relic and as the old-fashioned bulbs burned out the union busily scoured old army surplus stores for replacements. When the rotating mechanism finally wore out beyond the possibility of repair, it was replaced with parts from an old washing machine. They even sanded and painted the tower. But civilization finally caught up with us, in the form of vandalism. It became the thing to do for boys from Haverstraw to climb the mountain and shoot out the light with .22 rifles, though discharging or even carrying a loaded gun on state park property was a serious offense. If the park had ever run a single patrol over the property when the light was relit they would surely have caught someone, and put a serious damper on the sport. But that would have kept the beacon going, which did not suit their purposes at all. The suggestion offered by a cynic that it was actually the park rangers themselves shooting out the light has never seemed as far-fetched to me as it might to the casual observer.

Anyway, we came to the end of the line. The beacon would be dark for a week or so as new bulbs were sought. Then it would be on for a night or two, and out. Finally we were notified by the CAA that as it was listed on maps as an operating beacon we would either have to keep it going full time or give it up. The same people who had met in 1957 to get it relighted convened once more in 1962 and made the sad decision to let it go. This decision was scarcely announced before the Palisades Park people swarmed all over it with torches, cutting it down before some other act might save it. That was the end of our High Tor beacon, the beacon that so many had worked so hard to save.

8

The summer of 1958 was cold and wet, and the vintage was indifferent. Fortunately it was also small, so we blended part of it back into some of the wine made in 1957, and later blended the rest into some of the 1959. But a few things happened that year worth noting. For one, we had our first big story. Clementine Paddleford covered the vintage party, and unlike the abortive *Life* venture, this one was featured in the Sunday *New York Herald Tribune,* of recent memory. This worthy lady was basically a food writer, however, and she got carried away by all the casseroles the guests brought. High Tor Vineyards was mentioned as the locale, Alma and I were described as the owners of the winery, and the rest of the big and splashy story was made up of interviews with some of the lady guests and the recipes for their dishes. Our wine was hardly mentioned. The lightning had missed, and it was to keep missing for several years. Craig Claiborne came out in 1959 to do a story for the *Times,* but he too is a food writer, and the whole story was about how good a cook my wife is—which she is. When we heard he was going to have lunch with us Alma went into a frenzy of preparation. She bought a mold pan shaped like a bunch of grapes, and in this made a shrimp and white wine aspic. In each hollow representing a grape in the mold she placed a peeled and seeded Niagara grape, our grapes being too valuable to use in cooking. These grapes and the Concords she used for jelly came from the old vines around the house that have been here for perhaps a century.

We had recently installed a spankingly new and highly efficient electric stove, but Claiborne would have none of that. He had the photographer take pictures of her "making" the Concord jelly on an old wood-burning stove which we have used for warmth, but never for cooking. Then he had the photographer set up his equipment to record that awesome moment when the fancy aspic was unmolded. There is an old western superstition that if one takes a firm hold of the left testicle good luck will surely follow, but Alma is opposed to such melodramatics, so I settled for a rather prosaic crossing of fingers. She would have loved to do the same thing, but had need of all available fingers and thumbs for the ordeal ahead. The preparations were carried out: the brief immersion of the mold in warm water, the plate placed in position and the practiced flip. All breaths were held as the mold was lifted, and suddenly there it was in sparkling perfection. Even Mr. Claiborne applauded. Staring me full in the face as I write this is a large framed photo of this masterpiece, surrounded by fresh grape leaves and served with a sour cream sauce.

I suppose that is the price one pays for being married to a good cook. For the article was almost entirely a description of the food and a detailing of the recipes. There were three pictures, one of Alma making the jelly on the old stove, one of our house, and one of Averil carrying a basket of grapes on her head. It was a lovely article, but it sold almost no wine.

One of the most bizarre highlights of the late fifties happened on a day in late spring, just as dusk was setting in. We were going out to a latish dinner, and Alma was in a dressing gown, her hair up in curlers, listening intently to a record of some fey Frenchman swishing his way through the intricacies of French pronunciation. Alma is a great cook, as noted, but she does have something of a tin ear and I was purposely trying not to hear her earnest efforts to copy the voice as I shaved in the nearby bathroom. Suddenly her voice trailed off, and after a moment she said, "Everett, come here. Quickly."

I laid down the razor and went out to see what the trouble was and she pointed out the big glass window. "Look."

I looked, and saw emerging from the woods and heading down the vineyards toward the house three men in long overcoats, splattered with mud and totally bedraggled. I thought for a moment that we were about to be invaded by members of that Italian organization that you can't mention because everyone knows that it doesn't exist. I stared at them, and in the background the voice droned on: "Armand . . . Luceee . . . Jean . . . Pierre . . ." Shutting off the machine, I went back to the window to see if perhaps I should get the rifle. And then, incredibly, recognition broke.

The three men were the New York State Democratic chairman, who was also the state commissioner of safety, the local ABC commissioner, and the man who owned just about everything else in Haverstraw, where they all lived. The exhausted trio staggered into the house. After ministering to the alcoholic needs of two of them—the commissioner of safety didn't drink—I heard the following insane story.

It had been a beautiful day, and as it wore on the commissioner of safety casually remarked that he would like some topsoil and leaf mold for his garden. The tycoon said he knew just the spot on the property of the Palisades State Park. They could drive there, fill a couple of burlap bags and be back in no time. Of course the park was closed to the public and they would be trespassing, not to mention the thorny fact that they would technically be purloining park property. It was in Haver-

134

straw, and Haverstraw is not so much a township as a state of mind. To the old-timers all this was perfectly reasonable, and they got into the car without a second thought. The ABC commissioner went along for the ride.

When they got to the road entering the park, the road that says "No Admittance," they drove in, the commissioner of safety behind the wheel of his big, black, state-owned Cadillac with the special plates and the official emblem. But after they had driven a way along the narrow dirt road it became quite wet and soft, and the tycoon suggested that it might be better to come back in a drier season. There were tracks in the road, however, indicating that another vehicle had recently passed that way, and the commissioner of safety—a stubborn man—said that if anyone could drive along that road, *he* could drive along that road.

What none of them knew was that the tracks were made by a four-wheel-drive jeep, driven by members of the IBEW with park permission, to get a piece of heavy equipment as close as possible to the beacon tower we had struggled so hard to maintain. And even they couldn't have made it had not the jeep been fitted with a winch and a long steel cable. A man walked ahead, fastened the cable to a tree, the winch reeled in the cable, and the jeep was drawn fifty or so feet down the road.

The Cadillac was no match for the jeep, and it sank deeper and deeper into the mud as the determined man at the wheel forced it forward. Finally it settled in for the night. Everyone got out, and for the first time the predicament they were in if they were trapped there dawned on them. They began digging and pushing, tearing branches from trees in their frenzy to get the car turned around and back to the highway, but all that happened was that through an incautious maneuver the car almost went over the edge of a small cliff.

Now they were in it, and they knew it. The local daily paper was and still is rabidly Republican, and to have a photograph of an official car, emblem and all, of the Democratic governor's commissioner of safety in the most unsafe of situations, coupled with the fact that its driver was trespassing on state park property for the purpose of swiping some topsoil, could have had serious repercussions in Albany. They knew that if they walked out to the main road and down to Haverstraw someone most certainly would recognize them and want to know why they were walking and why they were covered with mud. It might, of course, be a friend. And also, of course, it might not.

The editor of the friendly Haverstraw weekly lived at the foot of the main cliff, and so this intrepid threesome made their way along the ridge until they were above the editor's house— several hundred feet above.

Leaning over the edge, they started calling, "Bill! Bill!" in stage whispers, but without a bullhorn they had no chance at all of being heard at that distance, particularly with the traffic of 9W rushing past Bill's house. It now began to get dark, and only one way out was left to them. That was to walk over the mountain from the township of Haverstraw, and down the other side to my house in the township of Clarkstown. At that time we were friends (I still am with two of them) and to make it doubly secure I was the newly elected chairman of the Clarkstown Democratic Committee; a member of the team.

All this was told to us absolutely deadpan, while Alma and I managed to keep straight faces. Then the tycoon asked to use the phone, and he called the friendly editor.

"Bill," he said, "you're not going to believe what I'm going to tell you so don't bother. Just listen."

It all worked out. Bill's brother drove up to our house and whisked them away, and late that night a four-wheel-drive tow car with a winch sneaked into the park, snagged the car from its perilous position and brought it to the garage of a good (in this case "good" means "organization") Democrat, where it was cleaned up.

I never made this story public until now, as I was a member of the team and I believe in party loyalty within reason. Also, I didn't want to hurt a great man, Governor Harriman. But it didn't matter. The commissioner of safety, in his other role of Democratic state chairman, later managed to lose the election for Harriman anyway.

The Clementine Paddleford article was the first *big* story about us, although as noted it sold almost no wine. But the first story that really affected us was one by Poppy Cannon in *House Beautiful*. We had been mentioned earlier by Tom Marvel in *Gourmet,* but briefly, and excellent though it is, *Gourmet* has a limited circulation. Poppy Cannon's very fine article was about New York wines in general, and for the first time we saw ourselves mentioned in the same company as the elite. Widmer's, who got the lion's share of the publicity, had High Tor Vineyards brought to their attention, and a couple of their top men came down to see us and to praise our wines. They were genuinely pleased to hear that it was a Widmer wine that first got us interested in New York State wines, and when they had the article and the magazine cover done up in a full-color reprint they sent us a bundle for our own use. And later, when we went through a bottle crisis, it was Widmer's that released enough of its own bottles to see us through. But wine people are like this. There used to be a charming man named Morris Sleppian who owned a company in Yonkers called Quality Fruit Wine Company. He used the same bottles we did, and as he bought them by the carload he paid a fabulously lower price. And he told me that any time I wanted bottles I should send my truck over and pick up as many cases as I needed at *his* cost. Unfortunately for all of us, Quality Fruit Wine Company burned, the company went under and Mr. Sleppian died of a heart attack.

The articles continued and we were mentioned in *House & Garden, Holiday* and other magazines of that caliber. We were also cited in books by Frank Schoonmaker, Alexis Lichine and Alex Waugh. (Waugh's book, part of a *Time-Life* series, was entitled *Wines and Spirits,* and in the section on New York we got a very full and favorable mention. Consequently we were asked to the cocktail party accompanying the launching of this book, a party attended by all the top food writers of the New York area. Seeing James Beard talking to Julia Child—and seeing these two together is truly a monumental sight—I went up to them and reminded Jim of the time he had forgotten a luncheon date with me at the Four Seasons. He remembered it well, and leaning heavily on the cane he had to use because of the considerable weight he carried at that time, he said, "Everett, all things considered it would have been just as well if I'd forgotten a few more lunches.")

But our sales were little affected by the publicity. We were a curiosity, our wine something one served with the statement, "Here's an interesting little wine I ran across recently." Well written as the articles and books were, they were largely read by people already interested in wine, people in search of esoterica. And the market for esoterica is a limited market indeed.

Nevertheless, these pieces were written by real writers, men and women who had won their spurs in the professional world of journalism. Most of them were essentially food writers and they tailored their articles accordingly. But there is another breed, the "wine critic," writers who have failed in every other field of journalism until stumbling into the lotus land of wine writing. They constitute only a minor irritant to the winemaker, but still they do the cause of wine in general a disservice. This is because they know almost nothing about the topic, and hide this from the public behind a screen of obfuscations.

A food writer writes about something everyone is familiar with, and therefore must be precise in his praise, exacting when he condemns. Overcooked, undercooked, too much salt, too little saffron, the shrimp was tough and dry, the French fries limp. Everyone understands these terms, because everyone must eat to live. Unfortunately, however, everyone does not have to drink wine to live, and it is very easy to invent words and phrases to convince the general public that it knows nothing about wine, and that these seers know everything.

When one writes a book it will be reviewed, if it merits it. And this review in most cases will be written in such a way that prospective purchasers of the book will have a clear idea what the reviewer thought of it. A person reading a book review should be able to decide for himself whether or not he may like the book, regardless of what the critic thought, for the good reviewer uses words which are a part of today's generally understood vocabulary.

The wine critic is under no such restraint, nor does he want to be. And because a true knowledge of wine is still so severely limited, and the number of articles the average general magazine will publish on wine so few, the "writers" who have crashed their way into this circle band together, protecting each other, closing the door on anyone else, their prose careening more and more deeply into the purple, their opinions and judgments into the unintelligible. Let me quote from just a few.

"The French say . . . a good wine, like a woman, should have pretty legs." "This wine is changing just since we opened it. At first I thought it was somewhat dumb; now it seems to be waked up and over-excited." "Flabby . . . burnt . . . vicious . . . smells of the barnyard." "Ropey . . . has good legs . . . tears readily." Do these words mean anything to you? They sure as hell mean nothing to me. When true wine men discuss wine they may use professional jargon, the same as lawyers, engineers and doctors. But it's not a put-on, and if something is wrong with a wine they can pinpoint it and put it in words with a dictionary meaning. For example, if wine has a trace of vinegar it will be discussed in terms of volatile acidity, something readily determined by laboratory test. A wine can be evaluated in terms of darkening due to oxidation, or corkiness, a flavor imparted to the wine by a poor cork. Sometimes small crystals appear in the bottle and then the subject may turn to tartration, the formation of potassium bitartrate (cream of tartar) due to the (generally white) wine's becoming unduly cold. Filter taste, caused by improperly prepared asbestos filter pads, will be discussed, as will a noticeable sulfur dioxide flavor, and this will generally be discussed in terms of PPM, or parts per million. But you seldom if ever hear a true wine man refer to a wine as being "waked up and over-excited."

We were interviewed many times over the years at High Tor, and we more or less knew in advance whether or not the resulting article would be accurate. Most real journalists keep notes, copious notes, and they will often return to an earlier subject after rereading what they have written. The most accurate article ever published about us, the article that finally brought us to the attention of the general public, was written by Vernon Groff, a member of the editorial staff of *The New York Times,* who had never written on either wine or food before. Precisely because of this, because it was all new and fascinating to him, he wrote it for the general public, for whom it was also new and fascinating. Not to wine buffs. Not to collectors of interesting "little" wines. He took pages of notes, and a week or so later called me to check on a couple of points he thought he might have confused.

Not so the wine critic, however. A few years ago a man who has since become the dean in this appalling field spent the entire day poking around the house, using up our time—and not incidentally our wine—and then wrote: "Mr. and Mrs. Crosby live in a comfortable modern house near the bottom of High Tor." Not surprisingly, this man had taken scarcely a note. He was just getting started in his murky career and the article was strictly free-lance. He sent me a copy and I jumped all over him for the inaccuracies, tossing in a few other gratuitous suggestions. He finally peddled the article, but he never forgave me. Another expert began his piece by saying: "Everett Crosby, Bing's brother . . ." This man had never even interviewed me, although he had been to the winery on two or three occasions. Let me make it clear that the only reason that I object to being called Bing's brother is because it isn't true. In all honesty the rest of the article, outside of an occasional detour into the purple woods, was quite good and came out on the credit side of the ledger. But accuracy is a fetish with me, as it is with any winemaker, and this slovenly approach to journalism genuinely bugs me.

The sequel to the above is that the first writer got even with us by not including High Tor in a survey of New York wines. There is no appeal from this sort of blackmail. If a magazine editor decides to do an infrequent piece on wine he almost certainly has no one on his staff who can do it. He must turn to this closed shop of half a dozen or so dilettantes. And because of the intensely personal nature of taste he must assume these men know what they're talking about even if he can't understand the words they use. The writers mentioned earlier—the Beards, the Schoonmakers, the Clairbornes, the Lichines, the Waughs—do know what they're talking about, and how to say it sensibly and simply. But they come high, and they want time to do an article properly. It's so much easier to use the know-nothings, and besides, there's a certain cachet about printing an occasional article that is presumably above the heads of all but the most select few. The fact that the "select few" consists entirely of this self-protective little group is not known to the editor, because the group makes sure that nobody finds out. It's really all so discouraging. . . .

9

The year 1959 dawned, as they say, clear and cold. Our family landholding business in California was in the process of being raided by one of those vultures who prey on small, poorly run family corporations. Ours had been about as poorly run as is possible to imagine, plus the fact that our family, in all its branches, was fragmented in its thinking and its loyalty beyond what is possible to imagine. So late in January I returned to the place of my origin to fight the good fight. Happily, virtue triumphed and the raiders were routed, thanks to some sterling efforts on the part of one of my cousins and her husband, and all ended well. I had time to go once more up to the Napa-Sonoma country and to visit, among others, Robert Mondavi and Louis M. Martini. Young Mr. Mondavi was still working with his family at Charles Krug and had not yet opened his own winery. I consider Robert Mondavi to be one of the most innovative and creative forces at work today in California, and some ideas he casually tossed out to me made an enormous difference in the quality of our wine. Particularly the use of glass- or plastic-lined tanks, and the fact that wine so stored builds up considerable bouquet, which previously could be obtained only by storing in bottle. I mentioned this the next morning when I went to see Mr. Martini, Sr., and I thought he would have a stroke.

"I take it as a matter of principle," he shouted, "that wine *must* be stored in wood."

Unfortunately, wine is not only a matter of principle but also a matter of hard and undeniable fact. And, as stated before, white wine is better off for not even having waved in the direction of wood, principles or no. But traditions die hard among old winemakers who have known no other way, as the son who is now running the Martini winery knows as well as anyone.

Perhaps here it might be in order to give a few hints on how to behave when visiting wineries. I am not talking about the guided tours run by the huge wine factories, but rather a visit to a small quality winery, particularly if your guide is the winemaker himself.

To begin with, there is an ancient bias against women in wineries, most of the reasons for which go back to Old Testament taboos and have no scientific basis. But there is a perfectly good reason why even the most sophisticated wine man will look with disfavor on certain women at a tasting, and that reason is perfume. A woman heavily doused in Femme, let's say, can quickly overpower and deaden the *fine bec* of even the most discriminating wine taster. The same is true to a lesser degree of some of the more pungent lipsticks. It has always baffled me how any woman who uses lipstick heavily can claim to appreciate fine wines, when every drop she swallows passes over a film of synthetic raspberry flavor.

Vastly more important than perfume, however, is the matter of smoking. Again I am not talking about the factories that expect casual visitors and generally provide ashtrays. But the cave, or cellar, or barrel storage room of a good, clean winery—and all good wineries are clean—has an indescribably lovely aroma, and this aroma is the same whether the winery is in

California, New York or Europe. To burn tobacco in such an atmosphere borders on sacrilege. We always had a No Smoking sign in the barrel room and the tasting room, and yet it was astonishing how many would say, "It's all right if I have a cigarette, isn't it?" What do you do? If you say no many will leave in a huff, never to buy your wine again. So I generally sighed and said yes, whereupon four or five others would whip out their packs, the fleeting aroma was gone and the tasting ruined for the nonsmokers; it would have lost its special quality. It's like tasting wine in a smoke-laden restaurant.

Smoking is the only gustatory pastime that actively intrudes on the privacy of others. If I go to a restaurant and have a martini and a half bottle of wine with my dinner I am not bothering any of my neighbors, even nondrinkers. If I drink too much and become loud and obnoxious *I* will quickly be tossed out. Yet if I sit down in a restaurant to a classically prepared filet of sole meunière and a light, fresh bottle of Muscadet, and the man at the next table runs through a pack of cigarettes, my dinner is ruined, and *he* will not be tossed out. The thoughtless arrogance of those who casually pollute the air that must be breathed by their neighbors merely for the sake of a momentary pleasure is hard to understand.

Drinking wine in a darkened wine cellar, surrounded by the lingering aromas of vintages past, can make even a rather ordinary wine taste superb, and is based on the same mystique as the "little wines that don't travel" myth. All wines travel, reds somewhat better than whites. What doesn't travel is the ambience. I have drunk with gusto a small country wine in the silence and eerie darkness of the Black Forest, or on a poppy-covered hillside in Spain, or in an Alpine meadow. Yet bringing any of those wines home and drinking them with a classic meal and out of the same glasses that have previously served me great wines would show them to be the innocent little wines they really are.

I have several times mentioned how desirable it is to call and make an appointment with a winery before dropping in. We developed quite sophisticated techniques for handling the casual visitor who simply wanted to "look around." But the late John Daniel, during the years he was running Inglenook, was the acknowledged master. Although I knew better, I tried to drop in there in 1952, 1953, 1958, and again that year of 1959. Each year I was met by what looked like the same Mexican, raking the same gravel, who told me (a) he didn't speak English, and (b) there was nobody home. No matter that one could see multitudes of people moving easily about in the gracious Victorian house near the winery. Nobody was home, and even if anyone was he didn't speak English.

There is something about the wine business that makes people think it is not for real. If one were a certified public accountant one would throw anyone out on his ear who dropped in unannounced to witness an audit. The same is true of a surgeon being deluged with nonprofessional visitors while removing an appendix. The making of wine is serious business, as critical and demanding as those mentioned above. It does not consist of happy revelers dancing barefoot in the wine vats, staggering from one bacchanal to another. But quite a few wineries encourage this picture and make rather a good thing out of the visitors. Loquacious guides will be provided who spellbind the neophyte with vast sums of misinformation. At the tour's end everyone mysteriously winds up in the tax-paid room, where it is suggested that a request to purchase a bottle or two might just possibly be complied with. If the barker has done his job well they all buy, and at retail prices. Berringer's used to run such tours in California, but with its recent purchase by Nestlé and the installation of the reputable H. Peter Jurgens as president there will undoubtedly be some upgrading. It is not comforting, though, to read that a "visitors' center" will be developed.

All the large wineries maintain some sort of guide service, in which visitors are taken around at stated intervals. Most of the small ones do not. I have often been asked to compile a list of wineries that it would be interesting to visit, but in these days, when the phenomenal wakening of interest in wine amounts almost to an explosion, it is not possible to keep up, and I have to rely heavily on an article my friend Charles Burck did recently for *Fortune*.

California winemakers are divided into the bulk producers, those who bottle their products largely in gallons and half gallons, and the premium producers, or those whose wines sell for upward of $1.50 a fifth. The bulk producers are largely located in the broad, hot central valley of California and are dominated by Gallo, the largest and getting larger; United Vintners, whose brands include Italian Swiss Colony, Petri and others; and, well back in third, Guild, a cooperative whose brands include Roma and Cresta Blanca. Right behind Guild is Franzia. These are factories turning out sound wine at reasonable prices, wines which are almost always a better dollar-for-dollar buy than most of the cheap imports.

The premium producers are located nearer the coast, where the climate is cooler. The districts are roughly four in number, although there is considerable overlapping. Probably the best known is the Napa Valley, north of San Francisco. To the west and just over the Mayacamas Mountains is Sonoma County, and north of that is Mendocino County. These districts tend to blur as some vineyards run from one county into the next, and they are generally considered as one district.

Speaking of the Mayacamas Mountains reminds me of a fine little winery named Mayacamas Vineyards, founded and run for quite a few years by a dedicated couple named Jack and Mary Taylor. I spent a great night there in 1958, and for dinner was served grilled robins en brochette. I asked the reason for serving such an extraordinary—not to say illegal—dish, to which Mr. Taylor said darkly, "I caught them eating my grapes."

The best-known wineries in this general area are Christian Brothers, Louis Martini, Beaulieu, Berringer's, Charles Krug, Inglenook and the adventurous Robert Mondavi. All these wineries are set up to receive visitors, even Inglenook these days, for Inglenook now belongs to the ubiquitous United Vintners. This brings up a new point, for so many of the larger premium wine producers are now owned by huge outside corporations. Almadén, the largest of the premium producers, now is owned by National Distillers & Chemical Corporation, Paul Masson by Seagram. Nestlé, as noted above, has bought Berringer's, and Heublein controls United Vintners, and by extension Inglenook. Inglenook was certainly one of the finest if not the very finest in the state, and when United Vintners took it over they promised to maintain the quality at that same high level. But when one reads that in the few years they have owned it the production has been increased from 54,000 to 225,000 cases a year one has plenty of reason to wonder. Heublein, it should be noted, also now owns Beaulieu. Christian Brothers, Louis M. Martini, Wente Brothers and a few others are about the only medium to large producers of quality wine that are still operating independently.

Across the bay from San Francisco, in the eastern part of Alameda County, is the Livermore Valley district. This was once teeming with vineyards and wineries but the steady march of development, like some creeping blight, has taken over one vineyard after another. There are still several premium producers in the area, notably Wente Brothers, Concannon, and Weibel Champagne Cellars, but the writing is on the wall. In the neighboring county of Contra Costa there used to be a small but excellent vineyard area near Martinez. A fine wine made from the Gamay grape was produced there by Joseph Digardi,

147

but some years ago the fumes from the nearby Shell Oil refinery began to make grape growing all but impossible. I see in a recent *Wines & Vines* annual listing of wineries that Digardi is still active, but it is credited with maintaining only one acre of vineyards. Presumably it is buying its grapes from other growers.

South of San Francisco Bay is the Santa Clara district, also being slowly dried up by the building rash. Almadén still has its headquarters there, but like so many others had been relocating its vineyards still farther south into what can now be considered the fourth district, of San Benito and Monterey counties. Let us hope that urban blight will succumb to whatever spray one uses for it so that this new area will have a chance to prove its worth.

In addition to the wineries mentioned there are many, many more worth visiting. Some, like Mirassou and Korbel, have been in operation for more than one hundred years, yet until recently were almost unknown outside California. But perhaps the most interesting phenomenon has been the number of small quality wineries that have sprung up in the last few years. To name just a few there is Hanzell, at Sonoma; the recently reopened Freemark Abbey, at Saint Helena; Schramsberg, at Calistoga; Heitz, at Saint Helena; and probably the newest, Chappallet, also at Saint Helena. The winemaker for this last one is Philip Togni, the guide Alexis Lichine provided for our tour of the top Médoc wineries, and whom I later ran into at Mayacamas Vineyards. I would imagine that most of the newer small wineries would very much appreciate a phone call before a visit.

The New York premium wine picture is dominated by four medium to large producers in the Finger Lakes area. Taylor—the largest by far—Pleasant Valley and Gold Seal are all clustered around Lake Keuka, and Widmer's is at the lower end of Lake Canandaigua. All these wineries are set up to receive casual visitors. The two new quality wineries in the area, Walter Taylor's Bully Hill Winery and Dr. Konstantin Frank's Vinifera Wine Cellars—both at Hammondsport—would probably appreciate a call.

In addition to these, Seneca Grape Products is producing wine in the western part of the state under the "Boordy" label through an arrangement with Phillip Wagner, who also continues to make wine under the Boordy label in his small winery in Riderwood, Maryland. In the Hudson Valley there are at present three wineries making quality wine from their own grapes: High Tor Vineyards, Hudson Valley Wine Company, and Benmarl Vineyards. Hudson Valley, recently purchased by Pepsi-Cola, is located at Highland, and I am told that visitors are welcome. In summer a staff of students is on hand for that specific purpose. Benmarl is brand new, having been licensed during the summer of 1971 and putting its first wine on the market in the late spring of 1972. It is the creation of my very good friend Mark Miller, who overcame many and varied obstacles in bringing it into being—not the least of which, of course, was bureaucratic meddling and rigidity. I would imagine that Mark would appreciate a call before a visit. And I need say no more about the visiting situation at High Tor.

To conclude this section on New York, most of the rest of the wineries—and some of them are huge—content themselves with bottling someone else's wine, or make undrinkable Concord wine, or produce that abomination of abominations, Cold Duck. I have omitted a few who are trying, but not being familiar with their products, I thought it best to leave them out.

High Tor was featured in another newspaper story, a good and accurate one by Robert Dana in the old *World-Telegram,* and it was mostly concerned with wine instead of food. But the paper itself was already in deep trouble, and the few readers it had left were not the sort to be influenced by a story on premium wine. One thing about the article that does stand out, however, was the mention of our two great dogs, Archie and David—Archie being sort of a foxhound, and David being all dogs to all people. A story could be written about them, and in fact David did write one, entrusting the manuscript to me shortly before he departed this earth for the happy sniffing ground. David was all brains, and Archie was all gluttony, and the only way to control him was through his stomach. Spaghetti was his downfall, and on certain nights when the ghosts of High Tor called him he would bark—and bark. He always stayed just out of reach, and the only way to get him into the winery was to make a small batch of spaghetti with plenty of garlic and get upwind of him. Instantly all sounds ceased and he was your slave. He would have followed you into the black hole of Calcutta if the spaghetti had enough garlic.

10

Nineteen sixty will always be remembered by us as the year of the birds. Why they came that year and where they came from I have no idea, but they came in such numbers and so devastatingly as to make the Hitchcock movie look like *Love Story*. One year they were a slight nuisance, eating a bushel here and a bushel there, the next they were swarming down from the sky, devouring over a ton of grapes a day. There had been a lot of building going on in Rockland County and many second-growth wood lots had been cleared. This, of course, dispossessed a lot of birds but there were and still are many wooded areas around. The eastern part of the county is almost all in state park and the hundreds and hundreds of acres of wild land are loaded with all the natural food that birds have always eaten. No, I think it was some sort of mania, something like the lemmings of Norway diving into the sea, or the local squirrels of a few years ago who jumped into the Hudson by the hundreds and tried unsuccessfully to swim across to Westchester County.

Whatever the reason, we were unprepared for the birds, and though I obtained some netting, set out flashers and exploded firecrackers, we lost well over half the crop. I remember once when we were picking near the end of a row and Alma called out that lunch was ready. The whole row had been uncovered, and only five vines remained to be picked. It didn't seem worthwhile to cover them for the half hour or so that lunch would take and so we left them. When we returned there was not a single grape on any of the five vines.

We called the county agent, who was as mystified as we. We called other wineries and got as many answers. Our position at High Tor is unique as far as birds are concerned: a small vineyard, brush free and loaded with particularly flavorsome grapes, surrounded on all sides by hundreds of acres of dense woods where birds can nest and raise their families, waiting for the moment when the feast begins. This is not true of the Finger Lakes, where the ratio is reversed, hundreds of acres of grapes being broken up by an occasional small wood lot. The bird buildup can never reach the point it does here, for the birds must support themselves until the grapes ripen and the limited woodland there does not permit it. Oh, I know they have trouble in the Finger Lakes. Such trouble I wish I had.

Certainly they have no such problems in California, where in many sections a tree is a rarity. Of course some vineyards in the northern mountains are pretty well surrounded by trees and do have trouble. I remember that at Mayacamas they had not only birds but deer as well who nibbled the shoots of early spring. We had that problem at first, but as the park at our back began to develop its property, finally putting in a large public swimming pool, the deer moved on. The few that still appear now and then seem undersized and stick pretty much to the woods.

It will surprise no bird lover that birds are true gourmets. If there is nothing else they will eat a Concord, making a face while doing so. But given a choice they will eat the hybrid wine grapes first, and not touch a neighboring Concord. I have a Seneca vine, a table variety developed at the New York State Experiment Station at Geneva. It has a lovely aroma, something like strawberries, and I like to eat its fruit almost as much as the birds do. I have tried to save some by encasing the bunches in paper bags, tied with string around the stems. On one side of this vine is a Niagara, and on the other a Concord. The grapes on these two vines will stand in the open, plump, ripe and inviting, while on the Seneca robins will be tearing off the paper bags with beak and claw to get at the fruit. Certain bird "experts" have told me this is impossible, as robins are meat eaters who never eat fruit. There is a short answer to this, which I will spare you.

There is no simple solution to the bird problem. Flashers are a total waste. They scare the birds for a day or two, and then they pay no more attention to them. Noisemakers are a little more effective, but still do not do the job. For two seasons I hung strings of firecrackers—cherry bombs, actually—on a timing fuse, interspersed at different points in the fuse so that they would explode at varying intervals. The birds got used to them, and I have seen small birds within ten feet of the shattering sound of a cherry bomb dart into the air, hover for a moment and then return to continue feeding on the same bunch. There is a carbide cannon that works on the same principle of staggered explosion which, I am told, works a little better. But one must remember that birds do their heaviest feeding right after sunset and just before and after daybreak. I had neighbors who did not appreciate the hour of 4:30 A.M. being made to sound like the landings on Iwo Jima.

There is a material made in Germany—it comes in a long rope of something resembling spun glass that one fluffs out over the rows—which is supposed not only to discourage the birds but to allow the full rays of the sun to shine through. Though it did this last, not only did it not keep out the birds but the glasslike material stuck to the hands and bare arms of the pickers in a most irritating manner. There is a woven paper netting coated with a plastic, rot-resistant material that comes in two four-foot widths stitched together down the top, and which one opens and places over the top of the rows so that the two sides enclose the vines. This worked fairly well, being light and easy to handle, plus letting plenty of light and air into the vine. But the four-foot width was not big enough for an abundantly growing vine and in order to fasten it under the vine you had to stretch it so tight that the grapes lay just inside the holes in the netting, easy prey for the voracious beaks. In vain I suggested that the width be increased to six or even seven feet. No one seemed to be interested.

Then Union Carbide got into the act by coming up with samples of a woven plastic netting that was guaranteed not to rot and was highly resistant to ripping. They agreed to make an experimental batch in twenty-foot widths, which I figured would reach from the ground on one side of a row, across the nine feet to the next row and down to the ground on the other side of that row. It was whoppingly expensive, but if it worked it would be worth it because of the fact that it could supposedly be used again and again.

Well, it didn't work the way it was supposed to. In the first place, the space between the two open rows provided a perfect flyway for those birds that worked their way under the netting or through an occasional rent—and there were more rents than I was led to expect in even the new netting. Perhaps this was the result of my taking the first twenty-foot widths that they had tried to run off, not having quite got the hang of it. In any event the birds, once inside, were in an aviary, completely safe from predators, feeding at leisure whenever the urge came upon them, and it came upon them quite often. In the second place, the netting ripped remarkably easily, and unlike the tobacco netting I will describe in a moment, which has cross ribs every so often to contain any tears, these rips would run on for six or even ten feet. The wind would blow, the netting would start to billow up and down, a section of netting would start to pull against a grape tendril that held it fast and pow! The rip would start, and run. And run. I kept the stuff, and when I was in need of a quick cover-up job I strung the whole twenty-foot width over a single row. Most uneconomical, but loosely bunched it was less likely to rip and there was less fly space inside for the occasional bird who managed to penetrate.

Tobacco netting, the first thing I tried, turned out to be the best solution for us. This is that cheesecloth sort of stuff the tobacco growers in Connecticut use to shade the plants that are grown there to make cigar wrappers. It seems that tobacco grown in the semishade has fewer blemishes and looks better on the outside of cigars. As I understand it, they use the cloth on the top one season, on the sides the next, and then sell it. For a good many years I bought it by the ton, sending a truck up to the Hartford area for it. It was comparatively inexpensive and if handled carefully lasted two seasons, an occasional piece for three. The width that it comes in, about thirty-three feet, allowed us to start up from the ground on one side of a row, down the other, across the ground between rows, up one side of the next row and down the opposite side. It was held in place by rocks—which are the best things that grow in Rockland County —down the outsides of the two rows, with an occasional rock thrown down the center to keep the netting from billowing up between rows.

That's the good side of the picture. The bad side is that it cut out an awful lot of light, which is why the tobacco growers use it in the first place. Grapes need sunlight to ripen not only the fruit but the wood, which must become hard enough to withstand New York's cold winters. If you put the netting on too soon you'll have a tough time ripening either, and if you put it on too late the birds will have already started their eating patterns and will get through the netting if it is at all possible. Generally it's possible. If you can get it on at the first faint signs of bird damage, get a few fiercely hot sunny days, take it off to pick the grapes and leave it off, and then get four or five weeks of good weather before frost, all is well. Anyone who has ever grown anything commercially knows what the chances are for this combination to occur.

I have heard promising reports on the use of ultrasonics and the highly amplified sounds of the cries of a bird in distress. What the cost of these systems would be and the amount of territory covered I couldn't say. The bird cries sound as though they might run into the same problem with the neighbors as the noisemakers, but at least these systems offer something a little better than a suggestion I received a couple of years ago from another grower. He told me that under emergency conditions it was possible to get a permit to trap the birds, and he was going to look into it.

"What do you do with the birds after you trap them?" I asked, an uncomfortable feeling already beginning to develop.

"Oh," he said. "When the cage is full you send a couple of men in with tennis rackets."

Of course. Stupid of me to ask.

Nineteen sixty was also the year of the last vintage party. It had been growing at an unmanageable rate for the preceding few years, but 1960 put the seal on it. For at least two weeks before Labor Day we had received an increasing number of calls asking when the "festival" would be held. When told that it was by invitation only the callers either demanded to be invited or said "You're kidding" and hung up. It might still have been all right if one of the local papers had not made a small reference to the "annual grape gathering" being held the following Sunday.

That tore it. They started coming early and they stayed late. All in all over three hundred people showed up, less than half of whom we knew. Of course they brought no food and dove hungrily into the casseroles brought by our friends. They wolfed down the wine as though it were going out of style, and quite a few got sick and redeposited it at inconvenient places. They stood around in great sullen mobs, waiting to be entertained, refusing to pick grapes, not believing that this was the gay festival they had heard so much about. As darkness fell there were still quite a few left, wandering around, feeling that somehow they had been cheated. Fortunately several friends also stayed and helped load them into their cars for the trip down the narrow one-way road. One of the drivers hit a projecting rock and banged in a wheel, stalling all the others until a wrecker could be brought to tow him away. He probably would have sued us but for the fact that he had left our property and the rock he hit belonged to somebody else.

Shortly after this, when there were only two or three cars left, another "guest" got into his car, fixed his wine-glazed eyes dead ahead, and without swerving this way or that drove straight into the brook. I had to get out the bulldozer and drive it, cleats and all, over the lawn to pull him back onto high ground. I need not say what the lawn looked like when it was over, and it took us several days to rake and smooth and reseed it.

We breathed a huge sigh when the last of them had left but it was not over. For weeks they kept coming back to look for lost eyeglasses, or to show the site to unfortunate friends who had missed it and who were determined to come the next time around.

Thus forewarned, in 1961 we called all our friends and told them there would be no party. We put ads in all the local papers, saying that the "festival" had been canceled and that the vineyards would be closed for all of Labor Day weekend. We had a young man, Carl Stensland, working for us at the time, not only a good man with grapevines but also a first-rate artist. If you haven't heard of him by now, you will. Anyway, he lettered a huge sign saying, "Winery closed for the weekend.

Please go home." Together we made a big stand and set the sign across the driveway, far enough inside the gate to allow room for cars to turn around and head back down the hill. Literally dozens of cars came despite the ads, and many parked and walked up to the closed and locked winery. We all stayed inside the house, peering out nervously through the shuttered windows until with the coming of dark the last car left.

Speaking of Carl reminds me of another incident at that never-to-be-forgotten last party. He had come to us from Greenwich Village, and with our permission had asked several of his Village friends to come and help. They were a well-behaved bunch and they picked their quota of grapes, but one particularly stacked girl chanced upon the swimming pool during the heat of the afternoon. She observed to a couple of my friends—males—that it would be lovely to take a swim, and they urged her to do so. No sooner said than she stripped to the buff and dove in, surfacing a few seconds later to float contentedly around on her back. Fortunately the members of the local press were on the other side of the house and missed the spectacle. So, unfortunately, did I.

Carl was the first full-time employee we had, and I am surprised that he stayed full-time after an experience we had toward the end of his first spring with us. Alma was up in the attic going over the clothes we had stored for the winter, and suddenly she came down with that expression of disaster on her face that generally means she has seen a mouse or some other dangerous animal.

"Everett," she said, "I'm probably crazy. But I'm sure I saw the tail of a snake sticking out from under the clothes in one of the boxes."

"You're crazy," I said, "but I'll look."

I had enough sense to be cautious, because with Alma you never know. I took a long stick and lifted the rest of the clothes. There, in plain sight, was a sleepy, but very much alive, fully grown and fully coiled copperhead. I went outside to where Carl was working with a long-handled lopping shears.

"Follow me," I said, "and bring that thing with you."

The snake was neatly beheaded, and then we looked in every other box in the attic. I am happy to say we found no more snakes, and we are puzzled to this day how that one got there. When the search was over we all went down to the kitchen, where generous drafts of "Wilson's—That's All" were downed. It is possible that the copperhead worked his way up through a massive silver-lace vine, and then in through a crack in the ancient siding. We promptly tore down the vine, but after that we always approached the attic with due respect.

Life became a great deal simpler after Carl's arrival. Time was beginning to run on, and the small ills that the flesh is heir to began to creep in. Gout is hereditary, and my father had it and his father before him. Thus I was not too surprised when shortly before my fiftieth birthday I developed it. Arthritis had already made its appearance, and washing barrels and walking around on the wet winery floor was not doing anything any good. We knew that Carl, with his artistic potential, would not stay forever, but we also knew that when he left he would have to be replaced.

The rest of 1961 was rather unspectacular but it was, however, a turning point, for we decided to see more of the Western Hemisphere. We had been to Europe three times, we had been to Honolulu for the better part of a summer, we had traveled by ship from San Francisco to New York through the Panama Canal, a popular way of going until Harry Bridges put a stop to it. (What an influence this Australian has had on America. When the last American ship ties up for the final time, and when the last American merchant sailor retires to Sailors Snug Harbor, I wonder if the boys will realize what Harry has done to them.)

We booked passage for a Caribbean cruise aboard the old *Mauretania,* and in the process saw quite a number of islands, one of them being Jamaica. And although we didn't know it at the time, this lovely mountain range jutting up out of the warm sea was destined to become our future home.

Many plants thrive in this tropical climate, but the grape is not one of them. A prodigal giver of its life forces, the grape-vine becomes an evergreen in the tropics, perpetually flowering.

In its constant struggle to ripen a partial crop while half-ripe grapes and opening flowers are on the same vine at the same time, it kills itself with overwork. I have seen a few fairly healthy vines in Jamaica at around two thousand feet of alti-tude, and I am told that anywhere above five thousand they can do reasonably well there. But grapes need a resting period, preferably a frost and a hard frost. They get by in southern California, where frosts are few and far between, but there is a definite difference there between winter and summer, unlike the West Indies, where the temperature hovers around eighty de-grees month in and month out.

On our return it was obvious that Carl was beginning to show signs of restlessness, and we knew that if we wanted to do much traveling we had better do it soon. I had always been interested in Chilean wines, some of which are excellent, and some—to be diplomatic—not so excellent. So we booked pas-sage on the *Gripsholm,* which was due to sail in late January of 1962 for a forty-seven-day cruise around South America, with a three-day stopover at Valparaiso, Chile. We figured that would give us time to see at least a few wineries, and if we needed more time we could stay longer, fly over the Andes to Buenos Aires and rejoin the ship a week later. It seemed a reasonable enough assumption, but this was the wine business, a business about which almost no assumptions are valid.

A few weeks before sailing I wrote to Charles Fournier, then president of Gold Seal Vineyards at Hammondsport, New York, asking if he could give me any help on whom we should see in Chile. He sent my letter on to Dr. Maynard Amerine at the

University of California, a man who is the acknowledged dean of the West Coast grape experts. Dr. Amerine wrote back and suggested I get in touch with Professor Alejandro Hernandez, professor of enology at the University of Chile at Santiago. I fired off a letter to the professor, telling him of our plans, and saying that if he had the time I would appreciate knowing whether such a visit could be arranged during a three-day stopover. If he felt there was not time to answer before we left, we would be picking up mail at the Canal on such and such a date, and a few days later at Callao, Peru.

We had heard nothing at the time we sailed, but that was not too disturbing. I was not even particularly concerned when there was no letter at the Canal. But I did begin to entertain a few doubts when there was nothing at Callao. Well, there would certainly be something at Valparaiso.

At Valparaiso there was no mail, and the Swedish American Line's Chilean agent said there had been no messages. A call from the agent to the university brought the information that the professor was not "at the moment" there.

There seemed nothing left to do but go to Santiago and conduct an on-the-site investigation. We hired a car and driver and set off on a hair-raising trip, negotiating the ninety miles in a little over an hour. The road was marked at quite close intervals with small wooden crosses, and when asked their meaning our driver said they each indicated a spot where someone had been killed. Once we passed a whole flurry of crosses, and were informed that two buses had met there head on.

However, we made it, and too emotionally exhausted to continue the search for the moment, we checked into the Carrera Hotel, which had been acquired only a few weeks earlier by the Hilton chain, and hence had not as yet been spoiled.

After lunch—and a nap punctuated by the hammering of workmen trying to convert a gracious hotel into a Hilton hotel—we again took up the trail of the elusive Professor

161

Hernandez. We went to the hotel desk and asked the clerk to call the university. The clerk looked at us in a puzzled way.

"But the university is closed," he said.

"Closed?" we asked in unison.

"The season, señor."

And then the whole thing burst upon us in glorious living color. We were in the Southern Hemisphere, the seasons were reversed from ours, and it was summer vacation. When I sent my letter in late December it was the equivalent of late June in Chile, and the University had just closed for the summer. Now, in early February, it was the same as early August at home. My original letter had probably missed the professor by a few days, a fact that was borne out later: a week or two after reaching home we received a most apologetic note from Professor Hernandez stating that my letter had arrived about a week after he had gone abroad for a summer vacation, and on his return he found that we had passed through about one week earlier. Hemispheric solidarity is fine, but you must always bear in mind which hemisphere you are talking about.

We were determined to visit at least one winery, and the hotel manager told us that while most of them were some distance away, Undurraga was within easy reach. Moreover, he knew of a man who spoke perfect English (he turned out to be an Englishman born in Mexico) who took people driving in his own car and who was acquainted with the people at Undurraga. He was called, said he was free early the next morning and promised to call the winery and tell them we were coming. You see even at the other end of the earth we knew of the necessity of calling in advance.

Of the many vivid memories of the trip one that stands out for both of us was that evening in Santiago. The hotel had a supper-club-type restaurant on the roof, and though I have now forgotten how many stories the building had, it loomed high over the rest of the city, with the traditional postage-stamp dance floor and a rather large outdoor swimming pool in which several tanned young men and nubile young ladies disported between trips to the bar. It seemed as though all of the long, narrow, partially fertile but more often barren land of Chile lay spread out at our feet, as we ourselves were at the feet of the Christ of the Andes towering in the silent mountains behind us. And the young couples splashed in the pool, the orchestra played the Latin beat of the moment, and on the minuscule dance floor beautifully dressed men and women stood locked together, making sexually oriented movements of the hips and feet. It was unforgettable and yet there was something ominous about it.

We were up early the next morning, and after our customary light breakfast found our driver waiting. He was a mine of information, and he told us in some detail of the economic conditions of the country. From what he said it seemed certain that a volcano was in the making.

At the winery we were greeted by Don Pedro Undurraga, who apologized profusely for not being able to take us around himself. He had an appointment of long standing in Santiago that he simply had to keep. Of course we both understood, for though a call had been made, twelve hours wasn't much notice to roll out the carpet and he obviously had wished to roll it out. But he had made arrangements with one of his men to show us around, and after a complicated series of farewells his assistant took over and we entered the intensely interesting winery building. And what made it interesting was not so much what it contained as what it did not contain. One of the things it did not contain was machinery.

Almost anyone who is at all familiar with Chilean wines has heard of Undurraga if he has heard of no other brand. This is a wine shipped to most of the other countries of South America, to Spain, to the United States, to Canada, and heaven only knows where else, yet is made and bottled under conditions similar to those of wineries at the turn of the century. The building seemed hardly big enough to handle the volume they must have been putting out, although it was quite possible that they had other buildings in another area.

As we entered the building we came into an area of large ironstone tubs over which ten girls were bending, laboriously scrubbing out used bottles by hand. Just above them was a fluorescent tube, and if the bottles looked clean by the light of this tube that was the end of the matter. They were rinsed again under hot running water and stacked on a small wooden pallet holding about fifty bottles each, which were carried by two men into the next room, where the bottling operation was going on.

This consisted of a small siphon filler sitting in a wooden tub to catch the spilled wine. The whole apparatus was set on the floor in front of an oval cask, with a rubber hose connected to the cask's spigot. The bottle filler did not have a float valve to control the flow, and the man filling the bottles squatted on a low box, controlling the flow by simply opening and closing the spigot. Several gallons of wine had accumulated in the wooden tub by the time we got there. The bottles were removed from the stacked pallets on one side, filled and placed on another pallet and carried by two more men about a hundred feet down a corridor to where a worker was sitting at a hand-operated bench corker of the most primitive design. The bottles were corked and still another team of men carried them down still another corridor to the bins, where they were placed for storage.

In another part of the winery, labeling and packing were going on. This operation consisted of a girl sitting at a table and spreading glue on a slab of metal with a brush. Following this she would wipe the back of the label across the glue-covered surface and place it on the bottle by hand. The bottles were picked up by still more men and carried to a table where the foil caps were put on with a hand crimper. Then the bottles were carried to a packing table where they were hand wrapped and packed, and a final team of men carried them to the shipping area. Perhaps thirty men and women doing the work that would be done in most other countries by three or at most four. This is not meant in any way to be a criticism of the wine, which is good. It is simply a commentary on the incredible amount of hand labor that went into its making.

Outside in the bright sun I asked our driver what the average winery worker received in wages, and he said one escudo a day. The escudo at that time was worth about seventy cents in U.S. money, and now it became plain why there was no mechanization. With those wages who needed machinery? We were shown the lovely homes of the members of the Undurraga family, surrounded by carefully tended flower gardens and smoothly raked gravel walks. Then we looked beyond the winery to the tiny houses of the workers, clean and neat to be sure, but company owned and housing Indian families whose workers received seventy cents a day in pay. We thought again of the well-dressed couples laughing, dancing and swimming on the roof of the Carrera Hotel. The cork was going to blow out of this bottle, and fairly soon.

Though English by inheritance, our driver carried on in the Chilean tradition when it came to driving, and got us to the coast in time for a latish lunch at Viña del Mar, the fashionable resort town up the coast a way from Valparaiso with its constant smell of fertilizer and fish meal. In addition to the lunch at the pleasant seaside restaurant we each took aboard a thundering case of *la turista,* a malady that kept us quite busy for the next few days.

It did not stop us, though, from marveling at the incredible spectacle of a passage through the Strait of Magellan. To us from the north the words "south" and "warmth" are almost synonymous, and we tend to forget that when one gets to the Strait the South Pole is thataway, and not too far, either. Though the sun was shining brightly—and the chief engineer, who had made seventeen previous passages, said it was the first time he had seen the sun shining there—the air was biting and crisp at a time of year that was the equivalent of mid-August. Sweaters were much in evidence as the passengers lined the rail to watch our ship glide past huge glaciers that extended from the tops of distant mountains all the way down to the sea. One could only shudder at the thought of what it must be like during the "cold" season.

The Strait itself is a maze of dead ends and cul-de-sacs. You will be heading down a broad, straight channel, confident that this one will take you straight through to the Atlantic, and suddenly the ship will duck into a small opening on the right and a most unrewarding-looking stretch of narrow water. Then it will open up into a broad inland sea, but that too is only an illusion, as the main body of water is left for still another small channel. A pilot is required for the passage, and our boat was under the guidance of a commander in the Chilean navy, taken aboard a few days earlier at Valparaiso. One can only marvel how Magellan ever found his way through this deadly puzzle with his small wooden sailing ships, no charts, no maps, and generally in the face of an opposing wind. One can also wonder at the emotions he felt when at last his ships burst out into the seemingly boundless Pacific.

We dropped the pilot at the bleak and remote outpost of Punta Arenas, at the very bottom of Chile, there either to await another ship from the opposite direction or to be flown home, for there was at that time no direct land connection between Punta Arenas and the rest of Chile. There was only one small rough road leading out, and it went up through Argentina, whence it was possible to cross the Andes and eventually get back to the main part of Chile.

Looking at the forlorn gray town, it was hard to imagine it as a thriving metropolis, but such it was during whaling days. Punta Arenas was the last place where supplies of food, clothing, gear and ships' stores could be obtained before going out into the Pacific for a year or more, and almost every ship stopped there. Sometimes the contrary winds would blow in the wrong direction for weeks at a time, and as many as a hundred ships would be riding at anchor in the immediate vicinity, many of their crewmen ashore for a last taste of "civilization." But these men had to keep a constant finger to the wind and woe betide a sailor caught ashore when the wind changed, for at the first hint of the shift the anchor was hauled in and the sails run up, and many a luckless mariner was stranded in Punta Arenas as the great race got under way through the treacherous straits, each ship straining to be first into the Pacific and in pursuit of the sperm whale.

The rest of our trip was rather routine, except that we found some excellent wines in Argentina and Uruguay. I suppose it is the preoccupation with beef that has kept these countries from pushing their wines, so they are unknown to all but a handful in America. And then again, in the words of that Confederate general, maybe Chile got there "fustest with the mostest." The other thing of note on the homeward leg was that in Rio we were taken to a nightclub by the parents of a friend at home. We drank bottled water with our Scotch, but forgot about the water in the ice cubes. Boom. *La turista* again.

11

We arrived home in early March to find that our premonition about Carl was correct. He was leaving at the end of the month, but as the pruning was finished and the vineyards cleaned up, things went along quite smoothly. For the first time in three years I went back to full-time active supervision, and with the help of two high school boys the summer passed without incident. But Alma and I both knew that it was only a respite, and that another full-time man would have to be found. The economy was roaring and men of the caliber we needed were not interested in what we could afford to pay, even with living quarters and full utilities thrown in.

Finally we decided to investigate the possibility of bringing over someone from Europe, preferably a man from either France or Germany who had some vineyard experience. But we were told that single men tended to be unstable and that it was better to bring over a couple. Also, vineyard workers were already at a premium in both France and Germany and those from Italy faced an almost prohibitive wait for the quota.

There were, however, quite a few young English couples interested in emigrating to America, and for them the quota wait then was nonexistent. We had, after all, taught the winery business to Carl in a minimum length of time. Why couldn't we do the same to a bright young Englishman?

So we went through a long list of dossiers given us by a local employment agency, and finally picked a man who had been a coal miner until the mines were closed down, then went to work in the post office. I deduced that if he had worked in the mines he was strong, while his post office work must have given him some insight into governmental red tape. His wife had had some experience in the management of a small hotel. All to the good.

We wrote to them and found them eager to take the opportunity. Papers were filed, all the clanking bureaucratic machinery was set in motion, and finally we were told to fork over $650 to cover the passage. Now there was nothing to do but wait for the couple's arrival. There would have been nothing, that is, except that the two men who operated the employment agency were crooks, who took the money and ran. You see, our couple was coming over to enter the wine business, so of course their arrival could not have been expected to go smoothly.

But though things at High Tor seldom have proceeded from point A to point B without stumbling over an unforeseen impediment, they almost always ultimately arrive. In this case the Rockland County district attorney, knowing that I was a loud and vocal member of the opposition party, went furiously to work, with the result that all the money was recovered. And so it was that we were notified in early January of 1963 that one Eric Greaves, one Anne Greaves and one miniature poodle, name of Tooty, would arrive on the *Queen Mary* at the Cunard pier on January 17.

A dock strike, as usual, was in progress the day they arrived. Not knowing what a couple from abroad would bring with them when pulling up roots and making the big change, I decided to meet them in our new pickup truck. But this posed a problem with the dock pickets, so I called an officer in the New York police department assigned to the dock area, who lived in my township. We made arrangements to be met outside the dock area by a detective, who would take me in through the pickets in return for promising that no freight would be in the truck going in, and only personal baggage going out. At least this went off without a hitch, and after parking at the foot of the freight elevator the detective went aboard the ship to locate our couple.

Now picture yourselves as arriving immigrants, poodle in hand, being hailed over the public address system: "Mr. and Mrs. Greaves, please report to Detective So-and-so in the forward lounge. Mr. and Mrs. Greaves, please report . . ." After all the trouble about their traveling documents, after all the business of the crooked agent, what else could they figure but that somehow they were to be shipped immediately back to England. Their fears were not entirely allayed even when they discovered that all Detective So-and-so wanted was to carry their baggage off the ship, bring them to where I was waiting, "reluctantly" accept the ten dollars I pressed on him, kiss them on both cheeks and send them on their way.

Eric caught on to the business quickly and in less than a month we felt sufficiently confident to make a two-week trip to Jamaica for a closer look, leaving the vineyards in his hands.

Returning to High Tor late in February, I found conditions ripe for a windup of the pruning we had begun before the wood had frozen too brittle to be handled. In the meantime, Eric had been practicing driving on the right, had taken and passed the New York State operator's test and could now deliver on his own. We finished the pruning by mid-March and then the four of us had a conference, for we had been making a slight bow in the direction of complying with the immigration requirements by having Anne do some housework. The High Tor house is small and most certainly did not need a full-time housekeeper. Both Alma and I like to cook, and a third cook in the house simply resulted in confusion.

So we sorted things out by deciding that Anne could get an outside job while Eric worked full-time for us. It was a good arrangement, and for the next almost seven years things went more smoothly at the vineyards than they had ever gone before, and most certainly smoother than they went after. Eric was strong as a bull, and because of his years in the coal mines he was an expert at building stone walls. Slowly the tumbled stone "fences" bequeathed us by the previous owners began to assume geometrical proportions.

The 1963 crop was going to be a big one, and as we had a fair reserve of wine on hand I decided to convert Eric into a salesman, and by the demands of the New York State Liquor Authority took out in his name a solicitor's license—fee of ten dollars.

I doubt if anybody can accurately define what makes a salesman. Maybe there are so many facets to the job that definition is impossible. But consider the case of Carl and Eric, both intelligent people, both dedicated to selling High Tor wine. Carl had come to this country from Sweden at the age of eight, speaking Swedish and heavily accented English. He was (and is) a proud and sensitive person, and the jeers he took from his eight-year-old schoolmates because of his accent determined him to master the English language. When I met him twelve years later there wasn't the faintest trace of Swedish in his speech, and in fact he insisted that he had completely forgotten his former language. But he spoke slowly, almost reticently, as though fearing a schoolboy barb at some Scandinavian reversion. He looked at the ground when he spoke, or he looked past the listener. By no means a spellbinder.

Eric, on the other hand, was glib and articulate. He had quite a large vocabulary, and he spoke all those words with the sort of British accent that should normally be counted on to impress liquor store owners. So what happened? Carl, as it turned out, could sell refrigerators to Eskimos, and Eric couldn't give away water in the Sahara. Why? Don't ask me. I haven't a clue.

Nineteen sixty-three was a turning point for many reasons, one of which was the way in which we made our white wine. In 1959 I had had the good luck to have a long talk with Robert Mondavi, in the course of which he outlined some of his theories concerning the vinification of white wine. Much of this was new to me, and out of it all came an idea that I was determined to try at High Tor. But that year the crop was small and only a small percentage was of really high quality. Three or four times previously when in need of enough wine to take care of my needs I had bought small quantities from Louis Martini to blend with my own, and I decided to do the same in 1959. For the last time I ordered several barrels of Martini's White Pinot, a fine wine in its own right, and a wine which I am sure Mr. Martini thought I was buying to improve my own. I hope he will not be too upset to hear that I was really buying it to stretch out what I considered to be a better wine.

Anyway, I decided to set aside the best of my own production and bottle perhaps a hundred cases as a vintage, something we had never done before because of the complicated requirements of the federal regulations, vastly tougher and more restrictive than those of any European wine-producing country. I am with our government on this, by the way, but I simply hadn't the confidence that I could sell a vintage wine at a higher price, and the mind-boggling restrictions hadn't encouraged me to try.

All vintage wines produced in this country must be made of grapes grown and fermented in the year the vintage calls for, not the 51 percent that is allowed in certain other countries. Further, this wine must be made from grapes grown in the same geographic area, and must be entirely fermented, produced and bottled by the man who puts his name on the bottle. Obviously the wine I had bought from Louis Martini could not go into the vintage product, and it wound up in the lower-priced non-vintage wine of 1959. The very best of our own crop was kept apart from the rest, was fermented and treated in the manner that I was determined to try out, and was finally bottled as "Special Reserve—1959" and put on the market at the frighteningly high price of $1.95 a bottle. Would anyone buy it?

They bought it. The one hundred cases I had were soon gone, and the clamor was on for more. But by law no wine can be labeled "Produced and Bottled by" if less than 75 percent of the wine was actually fermented and produced by the winemaker, and in 1959 only 68 percent of the nonvintage white was from my own vineyards. So I changed the label that one year and the nonvintage white wine said "Bottled at the Winery by High Tor Vineyards." It's interesting to note that not a single person noticed or commented on that change.

We were encouraged by the response to our vintage, made by the new vinification methods we had tried for the first time, and the next year we made a somewhat larger amount of vintage by this method, again with a big response. In 1961 and 1962 more and more of our white wine was made by this method, and the turning point of 1963 referred to earlier was the decision to make all of our white wine in this way. What way "this way" is I am not saying, for it took me exactly ten years to find out that this is the best way to make white wine from the hybrids. The new owners of High Tor Vineyards are entitled to this protection and I am in fact under contract not to reveal the method.

Yes, there will be new owners, but let no one shed a tear. The wheel goes round, nobody is indispensable, and if I was lucky enough to come up with a better way of making white wine in only ten years, who is to say what my successors may do? For us 1963 was a turning point in the overall acceptance of our wine. Until that year the red had always slightly oversold our white, but with the introduction of our 1963 vintage the white began steadily surging ahead until by 1969 we could never quite keep up with the demand. This does not imply any fall-off in the popularity of our red; its sales move ahead at the same ratio, year after year. But the white has now become so sought after that the 1970 vintage was sold out three months after it came on the market. And it is all our own. Nineteen fifty-nine was the last year we bought any wine from anyone else, and from 1960 through the vintage of 1971 not a drop of anyone else's wine has been in our bottles.

12

Nineteen sixty-three was a turning point in a much larger sense than the vinification of wine. Our only daughter, Averil, was married. She was in her final year at Sarah Lawrence College and pursuing at the same time a highly successful career as a model when she met one Tyler J. Smith, four years of Williams College behind him, three years as a Navy officer safely past, and just embarking on a career in Wall Street. Zowie!

I will spare you the details. Anyone who has married off an only daughter will know what went on. And on. But one thing that occurred at the ceremony is worth retelling. Our neighbor on High Tor, the late Earl Weatherford, was an absolutely first-rate church organist, and he offered to play at the service. The rehearsal had been brief to conserve the rapidly failing strength of an elderly minister, and Earl had never heard a Unitarian service before. So when Reverend Hayward—who had christened Averil 21 years earlier—said some words that were considered to be a cue in other denominations, Earl banged into the first chord of Mendelssohn. Reverend Hayward gave me a stricken look, I caught Earl's eye and slowly shook my head. The majestic music faded. Then, and only then, did the minister pronounce Averil and Ty to be man and wife. Two more bars on the organ and they would have been living in sin.

After the arrival of Eric and the departure of our daughter, there wasn't much more that could happen to us on the human scene that year. Knowing this, one of our four-footed friends took over in an effort to inject some spice into two lives that for the moment were pretty much spiced out. It took place on the very day of the wedding, when our huge half German shepherd and half probably collie decided it was high time to kill one of our neighbor's sheep. I really don't think he intended to kill it. It was just that he played kind of rough, and after frolicking with this particular ruminant for a while he became astounded when it failed to continue the game. I was called by the police the next day and told what had happened, and that Charlie had been saved from the firing squad by licking the hand of the policeman when he drew his revolver to dispose of the accused. I called the aggrieved neighbor, and after I solemnly promised that Charlie would mend his ways, he was returned to us. I spoke to the culprit severely, explaining that sheep in the suburbs were for the purpose of allowing one to indulge in a compulsive passion for rusticity, and should not be chivvied about as one would another dog or other useful member of the community. He nodded, and we had no further problem until, seven years later, led astray by evil companions, or perhaps simply following the relaxed morality of a time that puts the seal of approval on the killing of judges, he partook in an absolute massacre. Had he been human I could unquestionably have got him off by putting some beads around his neck and blaming it all on the environment. But he was not, and the decision was made to send him on a fateful one-way trip. He would probably still be here had he not had the misfortune to grow up as a neighbor to someone who insisted on raising sheep in what is essentially dog country.

The loss of Charlie was more than an emotional one. A better watchdog it would be hard to imagine, and wineries have need of such services. In a small one such as ours there are long stretches of the day when no human is around the bonded premises, and the constant locking and unlocking of doors is simply not always practical. Someone drives up, walks in, calls loudly, sees no one, shrugs and walks out with anything from a bottle to a case of wine. But not if a large, determined dog is growling in the entrance. I remember one night when a huge commotion broke out in front of the winery, which is about eighty feet from the main house. The winery was not locked, as the last thing I did before going to bed was to feed Charlie and then lock him in the building. I went out to investigate and found two local teen-agers, dressed in black slacks, black sweat shirts and black sneakers pinned against the wall by Charlie and absolutely scared to death. I called him off and asked the boys what they were doing. They had gone hiking on the mountain and got lost. Both dressed all in black? Both born and raised within less than a mile of the winery? Lost? No way. They had come up to steal wine or tools, maybe both, and but for Charlie they would have done it. I told them that had I not been at home they could have been in real trouble. They gulped and took off, and I had no more trouble with them after that.

Finally, in that confused and scattershot year, our professional friends took up where Charlie had left off in keeping our attention focused on the fact that life and the vineyards were an ongoing process. Dr. Frederic P. Herter and Dr. Charles Findlay (whom Alma always called "George" for reasons of her own) were wine buffs, with a small vineyard planted to French hybrids. Many a solemn discussion of vineyard care have I had with both about their thirty or so vines. And so when near the end of 1963 Alma began to have some disturbing symptoms, her local doctor said that she should be thoroughly checked by a surgeon. Dr. Herter (now Auchincloss Professor of Surgery at the huge Columbia Presbyterian Hospital complex) signed her into Presbyterian for a week of intensive tests. When they were about over, both Dr. Herter and Dr. Findlay came to her room and sat solemnly on her bed. Oh, boy, she thought, this is it. Well, let's hear the worst.

Finally, Dr. Herter cleared his throat.

"Alma," he said, "do you know how Everett prunes his Seibel 5279?"

These two are still very much in our lives, as Fred Herter fixed up my hernia about a year ago, and six months later Charlie Findlay removed from Alma's leg a growth caused by an overdose of sun. The community of interest between wine buffs never ends.

If 1963 had been a turning point, 1964 was probably the watershed year of our later lives, for two situations arose that made it necessary to think of our future in terms of more than a year or so. We had followed through with our plan to spend a longer time in Jamaica and had rented a house in Ocho Rios for January and February. And when we returned on March first, decision number one was thrust firmly and squarely in both of our faces by the welcoming committee that met us at the boat.

It seems that at a meeting of the *Obergruppenführers* of the Democratic party it was decided that I was the ideal candidate for Congress, and all I had to do was give the word to be assured of the nomination from New York's twenty-seventh district. Under normal circumstances I would not have entertained the idea for a second, for the incumbent was the redoubtable Katharine St. George, and even such well-known candidates as Bill Mauldin had failed to make a dent in the enormous plurality by which she regularly carried this heavily Republican district. But this was not a normal year. This was 1964. Remember?

I told the committee that I would think it over for two weeks and then give them an answer. It was tempting in the extreme, because I felt I could win. I have always been deeply interested in politics, and both Alma and I have held many party positions. Ten years earlier I would have swum in shark-infested waters for the opportunity to go to Congress. But this was not ten years earlier. I would be fifty-three in three months, and I had at long last to consider seriously what I was going to do with the rest of my life. Also, we had by now made a firm decision to buy property in Jamaica, and I need hardly point out that the winters in Jamaica are somewhat kinder than those of Washington, D.C.

The more I thought about it the more convinced I became that I could win. Much of the district was rural and I was technically a farmer. I was also a small businessman and I was beset by more bureaucratic nonsense than most of the voters. I could discuss farming problems with farmers, small business problems with small businessmen. I spoke reasonably well. But the real clincher was my strong suspicion that the Republicans were going to run Goldwater, and under those conditions I felt that at least six men or women in the district could win, particularly if the incumbent went all out for Barry—which, by the way, she did. The only burr under the saddle was that I really didn't want to win.

While all these thoughts were churning we received a call from Jamaica telling us that the piece of property we had set our hearts on was now on the market at a price that was within our range, but just. A guaranteed title could be delivered, and if we wanted it we had better act right now. Any further thought of Congress became academic. Alma arranged to fly down for a final check, I prepared to tell the party leaders they had better find another candidate, and this decision had to be made loud and clear. I called the county Democratic chairman, Dr. Richard Sullivan, and asked him to come over to my house to hear my reasons.

Dick heard me out, and I could tell from the mobile Irish face that he didn't believe a word I was saying. Nobody refused to run because of a fear of winning. There was some devious reason that he had not as yet fathomed, perhaps some special commitment, or an offer of patronage for a friend. Of course it was just possible that it was all some outrageous gag, and with that in mind he decided to go along by reversing it and throwing the whole thing back at me.

"Everett," he said, "you haven't a chance of winning, so if that's all that's bothering you, relax. I just want you on the ticket to strengthen the chance of some of the other candidates."

There followed one of the most ludicrous discussions of my lengthening life—a potential candidate refusing to run for fear of winning, and a political leader trying to get him to run by assuring him that he didn't have a chance. But I was on to Dick. I knew he secretly believed I could win, and I thought again of those cold, miserable winters in Washington. I thought of the commitment I would have to the party by winning, for one does not resign from Congress, and a winner cannot let the party down by refusing to run again unless age or sickness forces it on him. I shook my head for the last time.

"No," I said. "I'm not going to run, and that's final."

It was just as well I didn't, for my evaluation of the situation turned out to be 100 percent correct. The nomination finally went to John Dow, a fine man but one who had run for several less important offices and never come within waving distance of winning. But this time he won with ease, and two years later was reelected. He made an excellent congressman, but neglected to wrap the flag around himself to the required degree, with the result that in 1968 he was turned out of office by a demagogue. Happily, a story broke about the demagogue's nonpayment of federal income taxes, with the result that in 1970 John went back to Washington.

As it turned out, John Dow's election was a great help to High Tor Vineyards. The only maker of cork finish wine bottles in eastern America is Owens-Illinois, represented in the

New York City area by J. Rabinowitz & Sons, a firm dedicated to the eventual elimination of the small winemaker. My contact with them was a man named Volsted, and to anyone remembering the Volstead Act, the enabling act of prohibition, there was a certain consistency in having a man with so similar a name industriously keeping wine off the market. Because that's what he was doing to me.

I would call him and order bottles, he would promise to look into it and call me back. Nothing. In the fifteen or so years that I dealt with him, he never once returned any of my phone calls. So after a week or so I would call him again, and he would tell me that he had checked, and there were no bottles of the type I wanted in stock. I would then ask him when O-I planned to make some more, and he would say he would check and call me back. Again, nothing.

Toward the end of Mr. Dow's first term, I was in more than the usual bottle dilemma, as the entire summer passed by without delivery of the order I had been promised in the spring. As the absolute bottling deadline approached, I called once more and was told that something must have gone wrong with the order. There were no bottles. It was in vain that I pointed out that if I couldn't have the wine ready for the Christmas season I might as well go out of business. Mr. Volsted was extremely polite, but was explicitly clear. There simply were no bottles, and there was absolutely nothing to be done about it.

When I hung up I thought about the matter carefully. Owens-Illinois was in this case a monopoly, I was small business. By not honoring their commitment and forcing me to close was there not some antitrust problem involved? And what do you do under such circumstances? Classically you call your congressman. But it was even more classic in my case, for if I had not declined the nomination, regardless of whether I won or lost, John Dow would not be in Congress. I called John.

Such a flurry of activity as ensued I had never seen and was not to see until the same situation came up again in 1971. The administrative assistant to Mr. Dow called Albany and told the commissioner of commerce that one of his constituents was in danger of being put out of business by a firm licensed to do business in New York. The sparks started flying everywhere, and in a little over an hour I received a call from Mr. Volsted. He had a surprise for me. They had just located some bottles. No mention of the fact that a congressman had complained to the commissioner of commerce of the State of New York, that the commissioner had called Owens-Illinois at their Brockport plant, and that Owens-Illinois had called Rabinowitz to find out what the hell was going on. It was true that my order had been messed up, but it could easily be remedied by releasing some bottles to me that were standing to the credit of one of the Finger Lakes wineries.

You would think that would have solved the bottle problem, but the same thing happened last year. This time, however, Congressman Dow represented only that part of our property which lay within the town of Haverstraw. The part that houses the winery was represented by a Republican, Peter Peyser. But again luck was with me, as Alma and I have known Peter for over thirty years. So I put the problem up to him and told him of the spectacular success that John had under similar circumstances. Could he do as well?

As it turned out he could. When the smoke had cleared Widmer agreed to release part of its allotment to me, Owens-Illinois sent a man around to placate me, and Mr. Rabinowitz himself called Washington and demanded to know why Congressman Peyser was meddling in a private matter. I understand he was told why. A follow-up call to me by Mr. Rabinowitz resulted in several quite explicit suggestions in return, and prompted him to say that there was no need to use obscene language. Indeed there wasn't. But then, think of the provocation.

The other and vastly more difficult decision we had to make that year grew out of the first one. During the two weeks of deciding whether or not I should run for Congress, we had done more deep thinking about ourselves, our belongings, our very lives than we had ever done before. We had decided what we *didn't* want to do, but did we know what we *did* want to do? Our daughter was married to a man dedicated to the world of finance. By no possible stretch of the imagination would either one of them be interested in taking over the eventual operation of the vineyards. We had bought the property in Jamaica, and plans were already under way to build a comfortable house on a cliff looking out over the Caribbean, a cliff that rose above a small sand beach that was to be all ours. There was still no need to decide on the future of the vineyards, and yet the problem was there right under the surface, and we both knew it. Eric had been with us a little over a year and was by now perfectly capable of running things in our absence, which was why we felt no qualms about building a winter home in Jamaica. But Eric would not be with us forever. Would we find someone as good, and if so would we be physically able to train him as well?

The horrid thought of selling was not mentioned at first, but daily it came closer and closer to surfacing. Finally we knew we had to look at it squarely. We were both in good health, and except for the slowly encroaching inroads of my arthritis, active. We had no ties, political or otherwise, to bind us to Rockland County. True, we had our friends, but we also knew that if we made a new winter life for ourselves in Jamaica, we would have no lack of these as visitors. Finally, with Eric able to run the business we could sell to someone who did not as yet know all the ins and outs of the wine business without fear of its being run into the ground.

On the debit side of the possibility of selling was our love for it all. We had put fifteen years of our lives into it, and certainly the best fifteen. Without pouring out the treacle, it is perfectly just to say that next to our daughter, High Tor was the thing in the world that meant the most to us. Did we need to sell it? Did we really need to?

We worried this particular bone for several weeks, hoping that somehow it would get lost without our having to come to grips. But every night, long after going to bed, it was there, and every morning it was still unfortunately there. Finally we reluctantly decided that while we didn't *really* need to sell, in the interests of practicality we should. And so in the late spring of 1964 we called a friend in the real estate business, Carl Marcum, and asked if he knew of anybody who might be interested in buying a winery. The enormity of this request didn't strike us the way it should have, for asking if anyone would be interested in buying so specialized a business as a winery that was set up to make good wine rather than money was like asking if anyone was interested in buying a seven-toed giraffe with blue eyes.

We were therefore not at all surprised when "Quiz" Marcum came up almost immediately with a prospect, a psychiatrist. He knew almost nothing about making wine, but he had that slightly mad glint in his eye that by now we recognized as the true and authentic stigmata that Bacchus has placed upon the genuine wine buff. We showed everything to him and his wife and told him the price, which we now know was fantastically low. We were to keep eight acres of woodland, they were to buy everything else. This was in early April.

My first intimation that the doctor's grasp of the principles of commerce could perhaps be improved upon came in a letter dated April 27 in which he wanted to know why he should be expected to buy any of the wine made more than two years earlier. This, of course, was the treasure of the inventory. Indeed, the red wine made two years earlier was still not in bottle. I only wish I had had an inventory of aged wines of that size to pass on to our present buyer. But I answered him promptly and explained all this and negotiations continued. But neither the doctor nor his wife could seem to bring themselves to meet our price, low as it was, and the time dragged on. I do not believe in extensive bargaining, and when either buying or selling set an upper and lower limit that are acceptable to Alma and to me. Outside those limits I will not budge.

May passed by, June, and finally July. We had not talked to any other prospective purchaser because we liked these two and hoped they would make the definitive offer. But nothing had happened and on August 1 Alma went back to Jamaica to go over final plans for the new house with our builder. Most of the stumbling blocks were by now out of the way and we were only awaiting a building permit from the parish council of Saint Ann's.

It was at this time that the psychiatrist and his wife decided to make their move. They notified me that they were coming out on August 14, and I thought, "Well, I guess that's it." They arrived, and after some initial skirmishing they offered me five thousand dollars less than the asking price, and while it was within the limits we had set, it was just within. I must confess to being slightly annoyed that three and a half months had been consumed in coming up with a price we would have accepted in the first place. But nevertheless I said it sounded good enough to me. As Alma is co-owner of the property I could not make a binding commitment without speaking to her. In the meantime I, personally, accepted their offer.

That evening I phoned Alma in Jamaica and told her the news. She said it was all right with her and when were we to sign something? I said they were coming out in two days with a binder and a fountain pen, and she said she would arrive on the late afternoon flight the next day so that we would have a chance to go over the ground once more. I hung up and went to bed, happy at having sold the place, but unaccountably worried that we might have sold it to people who couldn't handle it. We were planning on building a summer house on the eight acres we had held out, and my sleep was troubled with visions of being perpetually on call in the winery.

So what happened? So next morning early I got a call from the ubiquitous Sam Aaron, proprietor of Sherry-Lehmann, New York's number one wine store. Had we sold the property? I told him what had happened the day before. Had we signed anything? Had we even shaken hands? I answered No to both of these. When was Alma coming back? Late that afternoon. Why?

Sam took a deep breath and was off on one of his sales pitches, something he does better than almost anyone I know. He can get you so confused in the first thirty seconds that everything from that point on is all downhill in Sam's favor. He had a friend, it seems, a friend who didn't know that High Tor was for sale. He had the money, he had the experience and love of wine that would take our beloved business right to the pinnacle of greatness. Furthermore, he would give us thirty thousand dollars more than we had just been offered.

I took a deep breath. When talking to Sam you have to take occasional deep breaths to be sure of having a supply of air in case you have a chance to say something.

Finally I said, "I've already talked to Alma. She is willing to sell. We have to give these other people the final word tomorrow. How can we see your friend before then?"

"When's Alma arriving?"

"About six tonight at JFK."

"All right. You pick her up and I'll get my friend and bring him up to Rockland County. We'll meet for dinner at La Provence at eight. Okay?"

I picked up Alma and told her the news. Alma is extremely ethical, even more ethical than I am, and despite a considerable number of political and family foes who would be extremely

186

skeptical, I consider myself more than averagely ethical. Who knows, but it's possible.

"You agreed to sell it to them, didn't you?"

"Verbally. But the property belongs to you as well as me, and you weren't there."

"But I agreed over the phone to sell."

"To me. Not to them. Technically there is an out."

She thought it over for a long time. "I suppose you're right. But I still think we have a moral obligation."

"Don't you think we've fulfilled that moral obligation by keeping the property off the market for three and a half months while they wrestled over the question of five thousand dollars?"

She sighed. "I know. But it's still not quite the same. They didn't go back on their word, and we will be."

Now it was my turn to sigh. "Unfortunately you're entirely right. But let's at least hear what Sam's friend has to say."

Sam's friend was as big a spellbinder as Sam himself. Some years later I appeared on the Barry Gray Show with him, Sam and Phillip Wagner's wife, Jocelyn. These first two were supposed to be trying to extract information from two successful eastern winemakers, but I think Jocelyn got on three times, and by sheer voice power I made myself heard perhaps five. All the rest of the show was a dialogue between Sam and his friend. And it was the same thing on the night in question. Alma and I said hello, ordered drinks, food and a bottle of High Tor wine, and then listened to the debating team speaking for the affirmative argue as to why we should sell High Tor to Sam's friend. Under the special rules set up for the occasion the team speaking for the negative was never allowed to state its case. In the final analysis I am not complaining, for the resulting decision saved us both a bundle of money. But it was a fascinating exercise just the same.

Dinner over, we all went to High Tor, and by the last faint rays of a daylight-saving day in August showed the place. When dark had fully settled in we took a bottle of one of our older red wines, the wine that the doctor had questioned me about buying, and went up to the house. Sam's friend waxed more and more lyrical until at last Alma and I agreed to try and hold off the innocent people who were coming up the next noon to conclude the deal. We slept badly, and if I had had trouble sleeping over the thought of being on call for the new owner, I slept almost not at all over the prospect that the "new owner" would probably not be the new owner, my agreement to the contrary notwithstanding.

If I were to ask Alma what was the most awkward moment in her life I am sure she would say it was seeing the doctor, his wife and a son climbing out of their car with a picnic lunch for all concerned, plus a chilled bottle of champagne. I think Alma would have called it off at that point, but I am made of sterner stuff. We ushered them into the house, sat them down, shut off their ecstatic comments at the first comma and gave them the bad news. They took it rather badly, as I expected they would, as indeed I would. There was no question of waiting. They were going to sign for it all now, or they were going to leave in high dudgeon, never to darken again the doorway of people who didn't know what the word "honor" meant. Et cetera, et cetera. And that's exactly what happened.

In the meantime Sam's friend began trying to come up with the scratch, something he seemed to have an unaccountably hard time doing for a man of his reputed affluence. Finally we came to the reluctant decision that he simply didn't have it and slowly the deal gracefully expired, much in the manner of the dying swan. High Tor was ours. Again.

Thinking it all over, everything that happened turned out for the best for all concerned. I know now that Sam's friend was of too mercurial a disposition to have continued long as a day-to-day proprietor of the business, and the doctor was simply not practical enough. As for us, we now knew that the price was vastly too low. The only one suffering a trauma was the doctor, but being a psychiatrist I am sure he knew who to go to. We treated him badly, and though we had sufficient technical grounds to kill the deal, it was still a fairly ratty thing to do. I am glad that it has not dampened his ardor for grapes, and that he now owns a sizable planting of the best sort of wine grapes. I like to think that he is happier now than he ever would have been with High Tor. Still, I cannot help but remember that if they had made their bid any time between April 27 and the thirteenth of August, High Tor would now be theirs, for better or for worse.

Basically, though, I think the deal fell through because neither Alma nor I was really quite ready to sell. I think we almost welcomed the diversion caused by Sam's friend because it took the decision away from us. It was sort of like deciding to have a beloved pet put away, and then postponing the fatal day because it's raining or the car isn't running well. When we finally did sell, we sold under pressure and tension, and I suppose that's the way to sell something as personal as High Tor Vineyards had become to us. Selling that way becomes a relief.

13

Although the vineyards remained technically on the market, we made no real effort to sell. The vintages of 1965 through 1968 were uniformly good, we made enough wine to meet the limited demand, we expanded our holdings in Jamaica, and all was well. It is hard, in retrospect, to distinguish one of these years from another, so smoothly did they go. Then of course—as it always is—the rug was pulled out. Eric gave notice and left us in June of 1969 to take up, with Anne, the—astoundingly—vastly more lucrative positions of butler and housekeeper. As such jobs offered almost three times what we were paying, not to mention food, free work clothes and in most cases the use of a car, we were in no position to argue.

The pruning and preliminary vineyard work had been properly done, and it was not too difficult to get through the summer with three eighteen-year-old boys who went through the motions of working. But both Alma and I knew that we could not hope to get all the vineyards pruned during the winter ahead. Nor could we hope to get another full-time worker at the price we could afford to pay, and we were certainly not going to go through all the red tape involved in bringing in another from Europe.

Once more we looked for a buyer, but by now Mr. Nixon's depression was in full cry, and money was tight. We did get a few inquiries from land speculators, and when the very good vintage was in we made a basic decision. Since it was highly unlikely that we would be able to sell to a winemaker in view of the rising land taxes, and since we were determined to hold out as long as possible against the developers, we would begin to phase out the winemaking operations, making just enough to keep the label before the public and the license alive.

Meanwhile offers from builders and developers kept dribbling in. Also an offer from people who wanted to put up a movie studio for the production of God only knows what kind of movie in this remote and secluded section of the world that was still within thirty miles of New York City. There were people who wanted to put up condominiums in that part of the property that lies within the village of Haverstraw and is zoned for industry, people who wanted to use the same parcel to build a metal-fabricating plant. In fact, just about every type of person in this world considered the property except someone interested in making wine.

It was at this time that our relations with the regulatory agencies took a turn for the worse. Possibly it was simply that our sense of humor began to give out at last when it came to dealing with these petty tyrants. Or perhaps they had become tired of the bother of auditing our increasingly tinier operation. Whatever it was, we knew that now we had to sell. No longer were we protecting a vibrant and loving friend; instead we seemed to be presiding over a wake.

As a prime example of what we went through with the authorities, consider a letter I got not too long ago. Is the collective official mind breaking up? I'm beginning to think so.

191

STATE OF NEW YORK LIQUOR AUTHORITY

Bulletin #441-(d)
November 3, 1971

RULE 16.4(e)—REVISED NOVEMBER 3, 1971

(e) For each item of liquor listed in the schedule of liquor prices to retailers there shall be posted a bottle and a case price. The bottle price multiplied by number of containers in case must exceed the case price by approximately 96¢ for any case of 48 or fewer containers. The figure is to be reached by adding 96¢ to the case price, dividing by the number of containers in the case, and rounding to the nearest cent. Where more than 48 containers are packed in a case, bottle price shall be computed by dividing case price by the number of containers in the case, rounding to the nearest cent, and adding one cent. Variations will not be permitted without approval of the Authority.

> STATE LIQUOR AUTHORITY
> ROBERT E. DOYLE
> ACTING CHAIRMAN

It's that part about rounding off to the nearest cent and then adding one cent that gives it away. Nobody not touched with a certain madness could have thought that one up. And what is the necessity for the rule in the first place? Simply to take away any possible freedom of action on the winemaker's or liquor wholesaler's part. If a man wants to sell one bottle of wine at one dollar from a case of twelve that wholesales at twelve dollars why shouldn't he? But the Liquor Authority wants to keep everyone in the same strait jacket.

Consider a bulletin sent out by the Minimum Consumer Resale Price Unit that began with the following deathless line. "PLEASE NOTE THAT CHANGES RELATING TO THE FOLLOWING FACTORS WILL NOT BE PUBLISHED BUT MUST BE SUMBITTED [*sic*] IN THE USUAL FASHION." It further stated that a reply must be received by the State Liquor Authority before October 1, 1971, at 5:00 P.M. Yet this bulletin was dated September 28, postmarked September 29, and received by me October 1, 1971. And all for something that said there would be no change in prices, and which in any case would not be published.

Or consider the federal people. In that same month of September, a month when every winemaker is furiously involved with trying to get his vintage in and under control, a bulletin was issued by the Internal Revenue Service, Alcohol, Tobacco and Firearms Division, and entitled "WITHDRAWAL OF LIQUORS FOR USE ON AIRCRAFT; RECIPROCATING COUNTRIES." This little classic stated in part that "the privilege of withdrawing liquors free of tax . . . for use as supplies (including equipment), maintenance, or repair, of aircraft registered in a foreign country is extended to aircraft registered in a foreign country only if the Department of the Treasury is advised by the Department of Commerce that such foreign country allows, or will allow, substantially reciprocal privileges to aircraft registered in the United States. . . . Corresponding privileges are therefore now extended to aircraft registered in the Republic of the Philippines, Netherlands Antilles, Dahomey, Ivory Coast, and Senegal and engaged in foreign trade." I need hardly point out the potential for the sale of High Tor wine to aircraft registered in Dahomey and the Ivory Coast, engaged in foreign trade. Also, I tend to look with suspicion on airlines who use Jack Daniel's or Old Grand-Dad in the maintenance or repair of their aircraft. No, I think my surmise is correct. Official minds are cracking up, and rapidly.

We stuck to our decision to reduce the inventory of wine on hand, and with that in mind we did not cover some of our more marginal fields and allowed the birds to eat the grapes. As I had foreseen, the proper pruning of all the vineyards was impossible, and we concentrated that winter on the varieties we needed most. We had taken in a young couple and allowed

193

them to live rent free in the small cottage in return for a full Saturday of work, a few odd jobs after the young man returned from work, and keeping the winery in at least minimal operation while we were in Jamaica. I did my best to show him the rudiments of pruning, but when I made my customary brief solo return in late March to check up on things, my first glance told me that it had been botched. Working against the time when the sap began to run heavily and pruning would have to be concluded, we managed to get perhaps two-thirds of the vineyards returned to a semblance of order, and decided to abandon the rest. Of the ten numbered fields four were left totally unpruned. One of these received the customary summer spraying and cultivating, but the other three were neither sprayed, pruned nor cultivated.

By now we were both convinced that we would never sell the vineyards to a winemaker. In our desire to keep the land from the bulldozer we finally came up with a rather desperate alternative. The land was offered to the Palisades Interstate Park Commission at approximately two-thirds of our asking price with the understanding that we could have the use of the houses during our lifetime. They could do what they wanted with the land. After our death it would all be theirs.

It was a wasted effort. It has now become painfully apparent that the commission is only interested in the appearance of Rockland County to the residents of Westchester County, across the Hudson. How it looks to those of us who have to live here is supremely unimportant. They have long considered Rockland County to be their own personal dumping ground, placing facilities here that nobody else wanted or would tolerate. And as our property did not have a river view and could not be seen from the homes of the multimillionaires who sit on the commission, they were not interested in acquiring it.

To justify the above attack let me go back to an earlier part of this book. You will remember that the New York Trap Rock

Corporation took its fight to quarry residential land in Clarkstown all the way to the U.S. Supreme Court and lost. As the stone on the land that could legally be quarried was about to run out, the owners sold to Martin Marietta for what everyone expected would be a mopping-up operation. Consider then the surprise when in June of 1971 it was announced that the new owners had concluded a deal with the park commission, under the terms of which they would turn over the only part of the Hudson Palisades that was still privately held in return for $250,000. The park commission would then hand this sum over to the town of Clarkstown in return for Clarkstown changing the zoning to permit quarrying of the same parcel of land that had been fought over all the way to the Supreme Court sixteen years earlier. All these "conservationists" would be saving was a hollow piece of cliff, gouged out from the back to the point where it is by now nothing more than a false front. And by saving this the company would be permitted to continue its hollowing out process all the way to the back of the great cliff of High Tor itself. The ugly gash already confronting residents of Rockland County would spread to the north, while the synthetic view would be preserved from across the river. High Tor and the palisade would become the biggest movie set in the world. Does the word "bribe" come to anyone's mind?

It seemed reasonably certain that only a builder would be interested in our property. But shortly after we both came up from Jamaica in late May for the summer of 1970 we had our first serious offer from someone who wanted to make wine. This is what prompted the decision to spray and cultivate at least one of the unpruned fields. And for a while it looked as though we really had a live one. What we didn't know was that price alone is seldom what holds up a sale. We have had at least five people who came close enough to our price to be acceptable, but one by one the options and the contingencies began to crop up that eventually killed the deal.

We worked with this man and a variety of his prospective partners through the summer and fall of that year, and finally it became clear that he couldn't or didn't want to swing it by himself and what he was really looking for was someone else to take the risk. This is a fatal way to go about buying a business, for anyone with the financial background to be invited into such a deal in the first place eventually asks the inevitable question: If this is such a good thing why don't you latch on to it yourself without any help from me? Once that doubt enters the picture most of the reasonably shrewd money men padlock their wallets and look for a safer investment, like a floating crap game or a hot car racket.

In the meantime the young couple we had on the modified sharecropper deal broke up, the wife effectively torpedoing us by leaving the day the vintage began. She took the family car, so her husband had no way of getting home after work and hence could pick hardly a grape. We brought in the small crop by dint of a lot of makeshift effort, and then made a similar arrangement with another young couple, who moved into the small house in November. But for two seasons I had been doing more physical work than I had been used to in some years, and a hernia condition began to worsen perceptibly. Finally it became so bad that I made arrangements for an operation to be performed in early December, as soon as Alma returned from preparing the Jamaica property for the Christmas tenants.

It was at this time that the new couple came to me and said that the husband had lost his job with General Foods. With my operation less than three weeks off, I offered him a full-time job, which he accepted. I went to the hospital and shortly thereafter to Jamaica, full of hopes for the future. There seemed now a chance that we would sell the property to someone interested in making wine, and now we had a bright young man running it in our absence. Ah, the folly of this roseate type of pre-chicken counting. For a more inefficient and a less dedicated young man I have never seen. I seriously doubt if anyone has.

One never knows when the lightning will strike, and certainly neither Alma nor I had any premonition on the morning of Monday, January 25, 1971, as we sat dawdling over a late breakfast on our terrace above the sea in Ocho Rios. But suddenly down the yellow gravel driveway a car came hurtling, and skidded to a stop underneath the allspice tree. And who should emerge but the Honorable Stephen G. Doig, the justice of the peace who had interested us in High Tor in the first place, who had lost his home to the thruway, who after some years as county attorney, and a term in the state assembly, was once more a justice of the peace twenty years later. Furthermore, following the death of his wife of many years, he had married a woman who had a house and business interests in Ocho Rios.

Steve and his wife Pat had come down for a week or so, and Steve had been reading *The New York Times* of the day before, which had just arrived. And there before his eyes, the lead article on page one of the second section, was the story of High Tor Vineyards, done by one Vernon Groff, and done as it had never been done before. Pictures, facts, enthusiastic quotes about our wines by people whose opinions mattered, and most of all accuracy. We read it through quickly and looked at each other. This, beyond any shadow of a doubt, was it.

I had known that some sort of article was in the wind, for Mr. Groff had interviewed me in December after I came out of the hospital. I had known that whatever he wrote would be accurate for, as I said earlier, he took copious notes and phoned me some days later to verify a fact or two he was in doubt about. But neither I nor Alma had expected this glowing tribute. If there was any interest on the part of anyone, anyplace, in acquiring a property for the production of fine wines, this would surely smoke him out. For the article mentioned that the vineyards were for sale.

Thus we were not surprised when the phone began ringing

about an hour later. Sam Aaron, who else? He had a dozen friends who would buy it in the next fifteen minutes. With Sam you never know. He might just have one. Then a call from Bill Sokolin, who owns D. Sokolin, the wine and liquor store that is pushing Sam's store for the title "Best in New York." I'm not taking sides; all I'm saying is that Bill sells more High Tor than Sam. And in addition to trying to buy the vineyards for a friend, both men were trying to tie up as much of our production as we would let them have. I told them to contact the bright young man. Again, alas.

By nightfall we had received seven phone calls from the New York City area to the island of Jamaica. We got another call from Sam on Tuesday, two calls from total strangers on Wednesday, another call from Bill on Thursday plus two more from strangers, and on Friday a guest arrived, bringing letters that he had picked up at the vineyards before coming down. Fifteen of these were inquiries about buying the winery, of which three were from people or companies we would have sold to. But most of this mail came from people who were carried away by the glamour of the whole idea, and who could no more finance and operate the winery business in the way it had to be done than I could dance with the Bolshoi Ballet. A typical letter was on yellow lined paper, written in pencil, and beginning, "I am a college student interested in acquiring a winery. Do you suppose that . . ." I prepared a stock answer to letters such as these and had Rhoda Williams, the girl who does all of my typing in Jamaica, prepare them in batches and send them to me for signature.

But, as I said, there were others. One of these came from Charles Millard, president of the Coca-Cola Bottling Company of New York. To get slightly ahead of the story, the interest generated by my reply led to two visits to the winery by top officials of that company. They already owned Mogen David, and now they were interested in getting into the quality wine field. After the second visit I really thought they were going to buy us out, but apparently a heated meeting of the board turned it down a few days later. All I can think of is that the Mogen David division, who would have handled the High Tor operation, panicked at the thought of making good wine.

Sam Aaron and Bill Sokolin kept restlessly calling me throughout the following week, and on that weekend another guest came down, bringing more mail. As personal guests come down for a week or two almost every weekend, this is the best way to keep up on our mail. Anything forwarded airmail takes five days, and in case the letter is the proverbial three-tenths of a gallon under in postage it goes by regular mail. This means it is shoveled aboard a ship in New York, any ship that may be heading south. Sometimes the first or second stop is Jamaica, in which case you are in luck. But more often the ship is bound for Capetown, and on its arrival there all Jamaica mail is put aboard a ship bound for Trinidad. But that ship may be heading for Denmark after leaving Trinidad, so the mail is transshipped from vessel to vessel until it finally winds up on one which will dock in Kingston. Three months is not an unusually long time for a letter mailed ordinary mail from New York to get to the addressee in Jamaica. This is not an indictment of the Jamaican mail service, which has no say as to how the letter is sent. But it is a continuing indictment of civil service employees and the arrogant way they treat those who pay their salaries.

In this second batch of mail were other important letters, including one from Harper & Row, asking if I'd be interested in writing a book. I was. Another contained the first draft of an article about us scheduled to go in the new magazine *Vintage*. This is the immortal piece which began, "Everett Crosby, Bing's brother . . ." referred to earlier. One of the reasons I didn't like being referred to as Bing's brother was that his brother Everett had been dead for several years, while I was alive and complaining. I made about a dozen corrections and fired it back

199

to the author, taking care to send a carbon to the editor. The piece that finally appeared in the magazine was most favorable on balance, if a little fey, and Alma and I both appreciate it.

But now we knew we were really in for it. For with this article scheduled to appear in March, a mention of the winery due shortly in *Look*, and a mention plus pictures in a *Time-Life* cookbook coming out in June, it could mean only one thing. Our dwindling supply of wine would shortly be unobtainable.

The calls and the letters continued through February, and then the expected began to happen. Sam called. Couldn't get any wine. Bill called. Couldn't get any wine. A call to the young man verified our thoughts. We were out of wine, he said solemnly. Out of white we would have expected, for we had only a few hundred cases on hand. But we were astonished to hear that we were also out of red. One should listen to the voice of one's astonishment.

What the young man did not tell us was that a price schedule he had sent to the State Liquor Authority on February 10 for the month of March had been rejected. It had been rejected because the printer had made a typographical error of one letter, and an item that should have said "Rockland Rosé—4/5 pt." said "Rockland Rosé—4/5 qt." What made the whole thing the epitome of irony was the fact that at the time we had no rosé wine in stock, and we were simply listing it against the time when we would have some more. If the listing had said 4/5 ton it would have made no difference. We had none.

The young man changed the *q* to a *p* with a pen and sent it in again. This time it was furiously rejected. Anyone should know that no corrections are tolerated on a price schedule. If we didn't know it by now it was high time we learned a lesson, and so the State Liquor Authority closed us up for the month of March. The young man was embarrassed to tell me of this failure, a failure not entirely of his own making. I only wish he had told me some of his other failings.

Now hear this. The lightning had struck on January 24. Liquor stores and restaurants were beating at the walls trying to buy our product, and two weeks after the lightning the SLA struck back by closing us up for the month of March because of a typographical error of one letter on the part of a printer, an error on a product that we were at the moment unable to supply. Now do you wonder why we believe a major overhaul of this whole bureaucratic madness is long overdue?

When we returned to the vineyards on April 1 the form had been reprinted, and we were back in business as of the day we arrived. Orders had been backing up, customers were accusing us of holding out on them and secretly selling to someone else, and now the flood began. The young man would go one way and I another as we scrambled to catch up on our deliveries. There was no time to take stock, no time to do anything but label bottles, pack them in cases, load them into the truck or the station wagon, and off to the races.

But a nagging feeling had been bothering me. In the bottle room we have ten storage bins, each capable of holding 2,500 bottles. When I returned five were empty, three had anywhere from one hundred to five hundred bottles in them, and two were reasonably full. You learn over the years to make a quick estimate of how much you have on hand—five single rows of bottles equals twenty cases, and so on. And it began to be borne in on me that the estimate I was daily making was less than the official figures showed we had on hand. So late in the month, at the first breathing spell, I did a complete physical inventory. It showed a shocking loss of something in the vicinity of 125 gallons, almost all of it from the bottle room. This may not be so shocking to a big winery, but to us, with only about five hundred cases of bottled wine on hand, it represented about fifty cases, 10 percent of all we had to sell until we could bottle some more.

The federal government requires a winery such as ours to

keep two accounts, one for all the wine on the premises, and another for wine that is in bottle and is ready to be sold. We are allowed a 3 percent loss during any year, and a 6 percent loss of all wine made in that year to take into consideration the greater shrinkage of new wine during its first year. Most of the loss is expected to come from wine in bulk, as tanks and casks sometimes spring leaks, wine evaporates through the staves of wooden barrels, and there is always some sort of loss during the bottling operation which is charged up against the bulk account.

But anyone who can add and subtract has little excuse for a large loss in the bottle account. You count the bottles when a bottling is over, and add this amount to your bottle inventory. From this you deduct your monthly sales, wine withdrawn for your family's use (two hundred gallons a year allowable), wine consumed on the premises as samples, and wine that has thrown too heavy a sediment and has been returned to the bulk account. For a winery of our size there is not much justification for a discrepancy of more than two or three gallons during any six-month period, and here we were with about 125.

Of course it was possible that some large sales had been made that had somehow not been reported. I went through the invoices—and by state law these invoices are serially prenumbered and bound in pads—and accounted for all but one. Checking the daily removals of wine on Federal Form 2050 against the invoices showed that everything balanced. Further, the ledger confirmed all this, and there was simply no way the loss could be accounted for by a legitimate sale unless the missing invoice represented a fifty-case sale to some store, an unlikely sale to overlook. We had been robbed of almost a thousand dollars' worth of wine.

I talked all this over with Alma, and we had the young man and his wife come to the house for a talk. They seemed genuinely shocked, and after thinking about it for a while remembered a night in January when the previous young man who had lived here came up in a rented truck to pick up the last of his furniture and had got stuck in the mud. The truck was stalled in the drive for several hours, and after trying to help him for an hour or so our young couple had gone to bed. Yes, the winery was padlocked. No, they had not changed the lock. Yes, they had taken the key from the previous young man when they moved in, but it was of course possible that he might have had a duplicate made.

We notified the local police, who came up and obtained a substantially similar statement, and then I wrote to the Alcohol and Tobacco Tax Division to report the theft. For not only had we been robbed, but no tax had been paid on the wine and the responsibility for this tax was ours and ours alone. Our winery is U.S. Bonded premises, and the unauthorized removal of anything covered by the bond is a federal offense.

As we had expected, two inspectors showed up in a few days to give us an audit and to try to determine what actually had happened to the wine. The loss was confirmed, although they reduced it to 104.2 gallons, they took statements from the young couple, and gave me a form to file, claiming exemption from the tax represented by the loss. I told the same story that the young people had told to me and to the inspectors, mailed the form in and waited confidently for it to be approved.

On July 10 I received the following letter.

Address any reply to	P.O. Box 15, Church St. Sta.,
ALCOHOL AND TOBACCO	New York, N.Y. 10008
TAX DIVISION at:	US TREASURY DEPARTMENT

REGIONAL COMMISSIONER
Internal Revenue Service
North-Atlantic Region
Date: In reply refer to:
July 9, 1971   AT:PT:T:ES
                            212-264-7027

Everett S. Crosby
D/B/A High Tor Vineyards
High Tor Road
New City, New York 10956

Dear Sir:

During the course of a recent inspection of your premises by inspectors from this office it was disclosed that there was loss of 104.2 gallons of wine under 14% in the bottled wine account due to theft.

Since you have not satisfactorily established that this loss by theft was not the result of connivance, collusion, fraud or negligence on the part of a former employee and/or your current employee as required by Section 780, Part 240 of the Federal Wine Regulations, you are liable for the tax as follows:

104.2 gallons of wine under 14% @ $.17 per wine gallon:

Tax	Interest from June 3, 1971 to July 22, 1971
$17.71	$.14
	Total.....$17.85

In view thereof, you are requested to forward to this office a check made payable to the Internal Revenue Service in the amount of $17.85. If the amount due is not paid by July 22, 1971, the interest will accrue accordingly.

Assessment of the tax will be withheld for a period of 45 days in order to afford you an opportunity to submit a protest with supporting facts, or a request for a conference to present such facts if desired.

Very truly yours,
Charles R. Harvey
Assistant Regional Commissioner
Acting

By now Alma and I were so sick of the whole thing that we felt we should pay the tax and forget it. But the more we thought about it the madder we got at being forced to pay

$17.85 for the privilege of being robbed of almost one thousand dollars. Finally, taking a full wind-up, I fired off the following.

Mr. Charles R. Harvey
Acting Asst. Regional Commissioner
Alcohol & Tobacco Tax Division
P.O. Box 15, New York, N.Y. 10008

Dear Mr. Harvey:

My first reaction to your letter of July 9 was to pay the $17.85 and get it over with. It would make a lively and interesting chapter in my forthcoming book, and a chapter's worth of material is cheap at that price. But then the obvious and manifest injustice of your determination has made me decide to protest what I consider to be an arbitrary and capricious finding, and I am so doing.

To put a few points in order, the loss was not disclosed during a recent inspection of the premises. It was disclosed when I wrote to notify you of the loss and the possibility that a theft may have occurred. Second, you speak of connivance, collusion, fraud or negligence on the part of a former employee. Nowhere in Section 780, Part 240, is a "former employee" mentioned, and the man who may or may not have committed the theft—if in fact a theft took place— had been out of my employ for at least three months when the event may or may not have happened. When I mentioned a "duplicate" key I meant just that. Naturally he turned in his regular key when he left, but that is not to say that he may not have had a duplicate made at any five and dime store in the county. Does one have a lock changed every time any employee leaves one's service, particularly if one has never had a theft in the eighteen years one has operated a bonded winery? Not one shred of physical evidence was ever turned up by your inspectors or by the local police that any current employee was in any way involved.

You say that I have not "satisfactorily established" that the loss did not involve a current employee. By the same token you have not satisfactorily established that it did. A major right guaranteed by our Constitution, and a cornerstone of the American judicial system, is that a man is innocent until *proven* guilty. Or does the presumption of innocence not operate under Part 240 of Title 26?

Finally, I have been operating a bonded winery, as stated above, for eighteen years, and never before have I ever exceeded the allowable loss, and never have I been subjected to any disciplinary action. All of your field inspectors will tell you that I have always respected both the letter and the spirit of the law. In view of this, your decision to throw the full book at me over such a minor amount does not seem to be justified.

Sincerely,
Everett S. Crosby

A long, pregnant pause followed, at least as pregnant as anything can get in the sterile surroundings of the Internal Revenue Service. Finally, after more than two months, I got a reply. The matter had been discussed at length between New York and Washington—$17.85—and as a result the commissioner felt that my reasoning did have some merit. I was, therefore, "directed" to disregard the letter of July 9. The matter was dropped.

Any sensible reader will begin to wonder why at this point we just didn't give the winery away. Believe me, this thought was discussed more than once. But I am stubborn, as Alma will gladly tell you. In addition to Coca-Cola, whose interest was in full cry at the time the loss was disclosed, we had three other prospects, any one of whom we would have been glad to sell to. First, there was a man with knowledge of the retail wine and liquor business who wanted to buy High Tor Vineyards for his daughter and son-in-law. They would continue it on the same minuscule scale we had been operating at, and in addition they would establish a small gourmet restaurant with six, maybe eight tables. Though this involved a zoning variance, I could not believe that it would not be granted. Our neighbors were so afraid of housing, which could legally be built here, that this variance would most certainly have been on the side of the angels.

Second, there were two young men, currently short of funds

but with impeccable backgrounds and references, who wanted to buy our label, good will, expertise and equipment. They owned land farther upstate which would be cheaper to maintain as a vineyard, the taxes were not so ruinously high as ours in Clarkstown had become, and room for expansion was infinitely greater. They would establish a vineyard on this land and build a winery. While the grapevines were growing they would use ours, and they would process them in our existing winery. Three years later, when their vines had come into minimal bearing, they would move our inventory of wines and our equipment up to the new location, and all of High Tor would again be ours.

This was a tempting offer, and if the young men's cash position had been just a shade stronger we probably would have taken it. For it would have meant that when it was all over we would still own all of the property. We would have the vineyards, which would have been brought back to first-class condition by them, and we could make the two hundred gallons of tax-free wine for family use. Plus the fact that if we wanted to we could continue to grow and sell the grapes at a break-even price and keep the land in agricultural use, and we would be free forever of the State Liquor Authority, and the Alcohol, Tobacco and Firearms Division of the Internal Revenue Service.

Finally, there was another young man, named Jim Cannon, an aide to Governor Rockefeller, but despite this almost fatal defect still a very nice guy. His problem was that as long as the "Guv" stayed in office, which may be until the year 2000, his job required more of his presence either in Albany or in Washington than the minimum time required to run a winery without professional help, and this he didn't want to do. So the stalemate continued.

In the meantime it began to be increasingly borne in on us that our young man did not want to work the way a vineyard manager must work. No way. We would hear his car trundle past our window at four or five in the morning, and after a nine-thirty phone call would find an exhausted, squinting bundle of resentment stumbling through the motions of working. Worse, he seemed to infect all the young summer employees with his special sort of spirit, or lack of it. At one point we had him, his two brothers and two other young men who had worked well for us before all at work in one field. Five strong young men, and the total daily output of their combined muscles was considerably less than Alma and I could have done a few years earlier. Why didn't we fire him? you may ask. A good question. In retrospect I can only say that we desperately wanted to sell to any of our three prospective buyers and we didn't want to introduce a new note into the negotiations. I mentioned earlier that perhaps the best way to sell something as personal as the vineyards had become to us was to sell under pressure, and by now the pressure was becoming unbearable.

I am something of a mystic, and an event took place in early August of 1971 that I now consider to have been a portent. Alma has an unvarying ritual, under the terms of which she has her first drink of the day at 6:05 P.M. On this particular day, as I was preparing the regular sacramental offering of vermouth and vodka, my mind somehow went back to something that had been bothering Alma for several weeks. She likes to tie the vines, something I cannot do because of the bending involved, and during midsummer she would go out between five-thirty and six in the morning and tie until about nine. But this season she kept saying that she felt something was watching her, not necessarily a person but still something. There was a gang of savage dogs running the mountain at the time, and we both thought it might be one of them. With these thoughts in my head, I opened the screen door to take the drink to where Alma was sitting by the swimming pool. As I let the door slam behind me I saw that she was motioning me to be quiet, but it was too late.

The pool is perhaps sixty feet from the house, and Alma,

who has incredibly sharp distance vision, had been sitting at the near end. The pool is forty feet long, and fifty feet beyond that the vineyards begin. The rows at that point are two hundred fifty feet long, and thirty feet farther on the heavy woods begin. Something was standing between the end of the vineyards and the woods, looking at her. It had a long tawny body, a square face and short upright ears. And when the door slammed it made a graceful feline turn, still looking at her, but by so doing showing the unmistakable long straight tail of a mountain lion.

Now mountain lions are among the world's most curious animals. In my youth we had a summer cabin on the south fork of the Trinity River, in one of the most remote sections of northern California. I had heard many a tale from the natives of being trailed for miles by a "painter," sometimes at distances of no more than sixty or seventy feet. Still, a mountain lion in New York State was a little much, particularly one within thirty miles of New York City. I tried to convince Alma that it had been a fox, but we had both seen enough red foxes around the vineyards to recognize one at the first glance. A bobcat? No, it was tawny colored, had a long tail. An Irish setter, maybe? No, it had very short hair, the tail had no plumes and the small ears were erect. All right, I said, not believing it. It was a mountain lion, a cougar. And I named it Xavier Cougar.

But Alma is trailed by a small deity that continually verifies her wildest assertions. Within a week *The New Yorker* magazine came out with an article that stated that there were in fact a handful of mountain lions—catamounts, they are called in the East—in the eastern United States. Although none had been reported even remotely close to our area, the article said that a season's range of several hundred miles was not unusual for them. And it went on to say that they frequented dry, rocky ridges. I doubt if there is any more dry and rocky ridge in New York than High Tor.

Finally I became convinced that it really was a mountain lion, and that this was a portent that something bizarre was about to happen. It happened a few afternoons later.

Alma and I were once more running over the logistics of running a winery with Jim Cannon and his wife. It was obvious that he wanted the place badly; it was also obvious that his wife wanted it not quite so badly. She wanted it, but she was cautious. In the midst of our discussions the phone rang, and I picked it up.

"Is this Everett Crosby?" said a voice.

"Yes."

"This is Richard E. Voigt. Is the winery sold?"

"Not yet," I said, "although we're discussing it right now with a prospective buyer."

"Don't sell," said Mr. Voigt. "I'm coming over one week from today to buy it."

I shook my head sadly and walked into the next room. Alma, Jim Cannon and his wife were going over the various cost items, and it was plain to see that we were standing on the very brink of a sale, a sale that like others before it might not be eventualized, but still an honest to God potential. Why these crazy phone calls?

"Who was it?" said Alma.

"Another nut," I said. "He's coming over next Tuesday to buy us out."

Everyone, including the Cannons, laughed. The number of people who had said they were coming over to buy us out would extend to the Sea of Tranquility and back again. But that "one giant step" always remained elusive. Money. The hard stuff. Scratch. None of them really had it. And now here was another. I made us all drinks, we lifted our glasses, and knowing the odds we all drank to another abominable "no" man.

I am sure you will recognize what happened. Richard E. Voigt bought it. On the promised Tuesday he unfurled all of his six feet seven inches from a Volvo, looked around, asked a question or two, breathed deeply and said, "I want it." He gave us his bank references, he wound himself back into his Volvo and he was gone.

Was he for real? Alma and I asked ourselves this question again and again that first night. But Dun & Bradstreet said he was for real, the Chase Manhattan Bank said he was for real. If he would sign the contract he was for real.

As the negotiations proceeded we got to know a lot more about Dick Voigt. He was thirty-five, in love with the good things of life, possessed with the enthusiasm and capital to carry his projects through. He was also one of those lucky people who can slip on a dog dropping and come up with a diamond. Consider. Shortly before the contract was ready, the bright young man who was "working" for us pushed me that half inch too far, and I blew in all directions, even at the risk of messing up the deal. But I am happy to report that his tenure with High Tor Vineyards is now one with Nineveh and Tyre. And at that precise moment, Father Tom Hayes, an ordained Episcopal priest, had arrived at one of those crossroads in life that one every so often arrives at, and when his lifelong friend Richard Voigt offered him the job of general manager at High Tor, he quickly accepted. Whatever else happens, there will be no more mysterious disappearances of wine that will keep cropping up in out-of-state stores to whom we could not legally have sold. I have told Tom several times that if I had had him working for me two years ago, I would have thought twice about selling the vineyards.

Finally all the details were worked out and a contract drawn. We gathered in my attorney's office to sign a document that would have been for the benefit of us all. Unfortunately for us all, Dick Voigt has an attorney who believes that he is not earning his pay unless he tries to talk his employer out of everything he has agreed to. Dick Voigt needs this sort of legal advice like I need advice on winemaking from Mogen David, but he had this attorney, and there was no way out. So when the dust had settled we signed a contract, a contract that should have taken any two well-motivated people about half an hour to work out. It took us from six at night until well after eleven, as every comma was removed from its surroundings, turned upside down and given a gynecological examination. But, like the aforementioned examination, there has to come a time when there remain no further extremities to search.

Alma and I looked at Dick Voigt, and all three of us slowly nodded our heads. At the stroke of a pen, High Tor was his.

14

Having followed the author through the trials and buffooneries of founding and bonding a winery, having followed that winery's development for twenty-two years, having been in on the sale and disposition of a going and respected entity, the reader is perhaps ready now to explore fully the author's opinions of the wine business as such—what's good about it and what's bad. As I always believe in ending on an upbeat, let's consider the bad first.

The pretensions, the chichi, the snobbery and the precious language have to head the list. Despite the best efforts of the California Wine Institute, wine is still a prestige item, something the average American brings out reverently on special occasions. There are first-rate jug wines which are priced to make them competitive with beer as a day-to-day drink, but the notion still persists that beer is a man's drink, wine a sissy's. The fact that wine is a man's drink in all the other major wine-producing countries of the world—and make no mistake, America is a major wine-producing country—is virtually unknown to the vast bulk of this country's population, all the advertising of the American wine industry to the contrary not-withstanding.

Outside of the strongly foreign-oriented ethnic groups, who in this country drinks wine in large quantities? Well, the winos, for one. I say this knowing I will be raked over the coals by such magazines as *Wines & Vines* for even mentioning the verboten word. But saying that winos don't exist is like saying the Mafia doesn't exist, and no amount of looking the other way will make either of them go away. Winos drink wine not because it is wine or because they like it. They drink it because a vagary of the federal tax structure permits the purchase of more ounces of alcohol per penny in a bottle of fortified wine—wine to which spirits have been added—than from any other source, and these desperate and destroyed souls know it.

A few years ago there used to be a small liquor store in Nanuet, New York, about three-quarters of a mile north of the giant Lederle Laboratory Division of the American Cyanamid Company. I have been in this store when the afternoon shift went off and have watched the cars streaming past, knowing that a predictable number would screech to a halt, the driver dashing in to slap fifty cents on the counter. Not a word was said as the clerk handed him a pint of white port, or muscatel, the cap of which the customer would be unscrewing on the way back to the car. It is a safe bet that the pint was half gone before the traffic light at route 59 was reached, a distance of perhaps another half mile. And that the rest would be gone before home was reached, the empty bottle tossed into the now vanished woods by the side of the road. Home to the little wife, not much to show for it on his breath, a tremendous jolt safely under the belt to get him through the single tame martini one has with one's wife, and the bottle or so of beer afterward with the TV.

Consider the following statistics. One pint—sixteen ounces—of 20 percent fortified wine contains 3.2 ounces of pure alcohol, the exact equivalent of four hefty two-ounce shots of today's eighty-proof whiskey. Almost the same as in four very dry martinis, and the equal of seven bottles of beer. All dashed off in ten minutes and at a total cost of fifty cents. These men were by no means derelicts, but were for the most part blue collar workers earning good money and looking forward to a better than average retirement and pension plan. That they were men of some discernment was shown by the fact that they had settled in the more desirable township to the north, else they would not have been going through Nanuet.

Now were these men winos? Under the present definition, yes. They were fairly advanced alcoholics who had done their cost accounting homework and come up with the same answers as their unfortunate brethren along skid row. The sin is not to call them winos; the sin is to call the abomination they drink "wine."

Second among the quantity drinkers are the young drifters, the forlorn and alienated rebels against society, who drink Chianti because it is cheap and because the raffia-covered bottles are decorative, and because beer is the drink of the hard-hats and is, therefore, unacceptable. The fact that most of this Chianti is dreadful stuff and is a vastly worse buy than any California jug wine is not important. The jug wines are the product of the American Establishment, and that also is not acceptable.

Another thing that is hurting the wine business is the pricing structure, and this goes back to the prestige concept mentioned earlier. It is sheer madness to pay five hundred dollars and up for a bottle of wine that will never be opened and is almost certainly spoiled should it ever be opened. I am not saying that a great wine, opened at the peak of its perfection, should not be approached with reverence. I have in my wine cellar several bottles of 1947 Château Margaux, 1953 Château Mouton Rothschild, 1949 Château Latour, 1959 Château Haut Brion.

But they are not held as collector's items; they are for drinking when the situation calls for it. The best of these, the three bottles of 1947 Château Margaux, are all that's left of three cases I bought in 1951, which cost me about three dollars a bottle. We had a bottle recently on the occasion of our fortieth wedding anniversary and it was superb. But I submit it was not worth the seventy or eighty dollars a bottle that is quoted in the more ostentatious of today's wine catalogues.

What has brought this situation about? Wine shippers and owners of prestige stores in the late fifties and early sixties learned that by ballyhooing the wine of a certain year they could pressure a great many people into buying it. Nineteen fifty-nine was the classic example. The season had been good—sufficient rain to get the vines off to a good start, hot dry weather in the weeks leading up to the vintage—in short, a storybook year. The word got out early that probably the vintage of the century was in the making, and even before the grapes had begun to ripen the shippers and buyers began bidding for the wine to be made from them. The result was that almost every drop of quality wine made that year in Bordeaux and Burgundy was bought and paid for while the grapes were still hanging on the vines. None of this wine would be available to the general public for three to four years, but the successful bidders had tied up enormous amounts of capital and during these years they were paying interest on it. The credulous public was panting to get at the wines, and the importers had no trouble in getting their investment back. In spades.

Thus began a whole pyramiding structure. Reasonably successful-looking vintages were bought earlier and earlier, more capital was tied up, and more interest was being paid on items whose prospects nobody really knew. As it turned out, 1959 did not live up to its promise. Too much perfection is never good for anything, and the season of 1959 was just too perfect. A little bit off here, a little bit off there; now the wine has to work to prove itself. Anything that comes too easily tends to be flabby, and this, alas, proved to be the case in 1959. For though the wine was of excellent quality, the perfect weather had reduced the acidity. Acidity, in reasonable amounts, gives character to wine, a hardness subdued, but just subdued. Nineteen fifty-nine lacked this, matured much too early, and those who bought it with the intention of laying it down for twenty years should drink it now if they have not already drunk it. It will not get any better and will never justify the price most people paid for it.

The ruinous practice has continued, and spread to high quality California wines. The frantic bidding has raised the demand for these fine wines, but it has also raised the price to a point that boggles the mind. One exceptionally fine California winery was happy a few years ago to have a distributor in Connecticut who could sell any of its wines. Now, with the competitive price bidding, this winery has given an arbitrary allotment of six hundred cases a year to the same distributor. Six hundred cases a year is simply not enough for any distributor to handle on a statewide basis, for his salesmen must take orders, his trucks must deliver, his office staff must price-list, and he himself must pay the state taxes and be responsible for the billing and receiving of accounts due. Six thousand is a more reasonable figure. As a result of the restriction the people of Connecticut will be denied an opportunity to buy this fine wine. And even if they had the chance to buy it the pricing structure has raised it beyond the means of all but a limited few, and these few are generally not genuine wine lovers, but wine snobs. In the immortal words of James Thurber, "It's a naïve domestic Burgundy without any breeding, but I think you'll be amused by its presumption."

Also on the negative side of the wine business is the continuing trend of small prestige wineries being bought up by the huge conglomerates. This cannot possibly result in anything but the downgrading of wines that previously were proudly made and proudly sold. If National Distillers owns several brands that previously competed among themselves for the quality market, the reason for such competition is now gone. A certain standardization will be inevitable, much the same as General Motors uses many interchangeable body and engine parts on all its models, from Chevrolet to Cadillac. If one discounts American Motors, the competition for the automobile market is limited to three giants, and the quality wine business is shaping up the same way. The imports have their share of the automobile market just as the imports have their share of the wine market, and it is not inconceivable that the independent makers of quality American wine may someday go the same route as the Pierce Arrow, the Marmon and the Packard.

Now, of course, we come to that pervading evil of the wine business—government interference. Alcoholic beverages were once illegal, and though almost forty years have gone by since the repeal of prohibition, both federal and state governments operate on the theory that it is still illegal. They consider themselves to be doing you a favor by grudgingly allowing you to operate on the shadowy fringes of legality through the imposition of the most insane set of strictures and regulations ever thought up by the mind of man. And their interference is in inverse ratio to the size of the winemaking operation. If you are a giant you will have clerks and secretaries who do nothing but thread their daily ways through the maze of regulations. You will have plant foremen who can handle a federal audit, you will have computers programmed to anticipate the next bureaucratic idiocy. But the smooth flow of the winery's operation proceeds with scarcely a ripple.

If, however, you are High Tor Vineyards, you are clerk, secretary, plant foreman, vineyard manager and computer rolled into one harried person. Any time an inspector drops in for an unannounced audit everything else grinds to a halt. Never mind that you had planned to bottle, deliver or, indeed, play golf. You are his to command as long as he plans on staying—and you would be surprised how long most of them plan on staying. It is, after all, a most pleasant place.

A story told me by an inspector long since retired illustrates dramatically the inverse amount of interference that I referred to. It seems that a small maker of fruit wines decided to produce a cherry wine in the same way that it was made in the country he came from. According to my inspector friend—and he is a friend—most of the definitive cherry flavor comes from the pit and not from the fruit. Consequently, small amounts of cherry pits are ground up and added to the wine during the fermenting and aging periods, after which the wine is filtered and bottled. But the Alcohol and Tobacco Tax Unit decided that this constituted adulteration, and clamped down on the operation. Every bottle of cherry wine, said the inspector, that enters this country from abroad is made with the use of ground-up cherry pits, and on this basis the baffled fruit-wine maker appealed the decision.

"He's entirely right," said the inspector. "Unfortunately, however, he's going to lose."

He did, and eventually went bankrupt. In the meantime thousands of cases of cherry wine made by the method denied to him were and are being imported from Denmark, Holland and elsewhere because they are accompanied by a certificate of approval from the government involved. The Alcohol and Tobacco Tax Unit knew all this, but preferred putting a small winemaker out of business to bending a rule. Had he been a giant he would have hired a battery of high-powered lawyers who would have gone to Washington and made oblique remarks to certain officials about a congressional investigation concerning discriminatory practices affecting an American taxpayer. The rule would have been bent.

Consider New York, a state ranking second only to California in the production of American wine. Granted the gap between number one and number two is enormous, but still the wine business is extremely important to New York's economy. So what does the Empire State do? It charges a flat winery license fee for all wineries, large or small. If you are a giant selling a million or more cases of wine a year you pay $768.75 each year for your license. If you are High Tor Vineyards and selling one thousand cases a year you pay the same price. You are closed up for typographical errors that a large winery would have the staff to catch and correct, you are told that if you want to sell split cases at the same price as a case of one kind to assist some of your smaller customers you may not do so, while at the same time you are told that you may not establish a minimum number of cases for a long-distance delivery because this constitutes discrimination against your smaller customers—the same people you were trying to help by the previous request that was denied. It all goes back to the old prohibition syndrome. If you aren't a crook, what are you doing in the wine business, and the sooner we put you out of it the better off we'll all be. This in the number two wine-producing state in the nation.

After this catalogue of ills some people may find it hard to believe that there is anything *good* about the wine business. But there are good things, many good things. Foremost is the community of interest between true wine people, something that simply cannot be described. With rare exceptions winemakers try to help each other when confronted by problems. As I have said several times before, there is a ritualistic feeling about winemaking that makes its practitioners approach it almost as a religion. When Louis Martini said, "I take it as a matter of principle that wine *must* be stored in wood," he could just as easily have substituted the word "faith" for "principle." When Henri Gouge solemnly intoned, *"Les hybrides ne sont pas nobles,"* he was simply running through the catechism. We read of ancient Greeks returning after long years abroad, and gazing first with affection upon their vineyard and after that upon their house. It is this ongoing involvement with antiquity that makes us all feel honored to be trusted with a tiny fragment of its history. Whether this feeling will continue after American winemaking is divided, like Gaul, into three parts—National Distillers, Heublein and Nestlé—remains to be seen.

Another good or perhaps encouraging aspect of the wine business is the fact that wine has more and more come to be accepted as a food, an ingredient in a meal. Most states now permit table wines—wines under 14 percent alcohol by volume—to be bought in supermarkets, so that if the food buyer decides on a standing rib roast the accompanying hearty red wine is right there to go with it. Naturally New York is not one of these states, and after purchasing the roast one must sometimes drive several miles to a liquor store for the wine. Beer you can get at the supermarket, and so beer is what people drink.

What may finally overcome the chichi status of wine, what may get it out of the catalogues and onto the tables, what may in fact thwart the creeping monopolies, is the tremendous growth of home winemaking—caused in part by spiraling wine prices that the catalogue purveyors brought about. All over the country chains of shops are springing up that cater to winemakers' needs. Twenty years ago there was not a place outside the big metropolitan centers—sometimes not even there—where you could buy such simple items as saccharometers, acid testers, sulfur strips or simple corking machines. Now they are everywhere. But what has brought winemaking within the reach of the rawest novice is the wide availability of quality grape concentrates. It goes without saying that you can always make something better by using high quality natural ingredients than by using substitutes, and thus a well-made wine from quality grapes will always be better than a well-made wine from concentrates. But on the other hand, a well-made wine from concentrates will be better than a well-made wine from inferior grapes, and it is easier to make. And high quality wine grapes are simply not to be had in many parts of this country. Unless you live in or near California and can get Cabernet, or Pinot noir, or Riesling, or even mountain-grown Zinfandel, forget it. The same applies in the East unless you live near someone who grows the hybrids and can be wheedled into selling some. It is true that tons of California wine grapes find their way into the eastern market each fall, but these are grown in the hot central valley, are high in sugar and low in acid, and tend to make an undistinguished wine. And I think by now the reader knows how I feel about Concords.

What this is leading to is that many people who have achieved success in making wine through this substitute method get the itch to make the real thing, and wherever space permits are planting small vineyards. Over the last few years a steady and increasing number of letters has been coming to me requesting information on the hybrids. My friends in the nursery business tell me that sales of these varieties in small lots have gone up tremendously, as more and more enthusiasts are setting out vineyards of twenty to one hundred vines. In the case of beer, you can make a perfectly drinkable variety out of malt extract and a much better one through the use of true barley malt, and after starting with the first the true perfectionist goes on to the second. So it is with wine.

The wine man never really retires from his business. Cattle ranchers, publishers, shoe manufacturers retire to hobbies generally remote from their professional pursuits; winemakers do not. While breath remains they will find some way to attend the mysterious ceremonies connected with the fermentation and vinification of the grape. Consider. I have sold High Tor Vineyards, and by the terms of the contract I can never again become involved with commercial winemaking. I live in Jamaica, where the grape does not grow. But I have recently completed, largely with my own hands, a small air-conditioned wine cellar facing the sea, complete with storage bins and worktable for the production of wine through the use of concentrates. I might also say that I have been turning out some eminently drinkable beer, and turning it out for pennies a bottle.

But though we live in Jamaica most of the year, Alma and I have recently bought a summer house and four acres of land sloping down toward the Hudson River, just one hundred miles north of High Tor. We have already ordered an initial planting of eighty grapevines, and they will go into the ground in the spring of 1973. The house itself has a spacious, cool and well-drained cellar, and I have drawn up plans showing the location of the worktables, the storage bins, the sink and other necessary paraphernalia of successful winemaking. We are enthusiastically rounding up pieces of equipment lent out over the years to friends, even including the first crusher and press ever used at High Tor Vineyards. We are looking forward to our first small vintage of 1975, and it will be as carefully and reverently handled as any at High Tor. When we are in full production we will make between forty and fifty gallons of wine a year for our own use, and we will make it free of the dead hand of government.

To me the good has always outweighed the bad as far as the wine business goes, or I would not have stayed with it. It can be as good as one has the stamina to make it, and if one does not have the stamina it can be as bad as it is possible to imagine. It would be a better business if the government devoted less time to crippling regulations and gave at least a little thought to the creeping cartelization that is taking over the industry. It would be a better business if people could be persuaded to stop bowing before the meaningless word "imported." Finally, it would be a much better business if everyone, the regulatory officials as well as the potential consumers, could be convinced that table wine is the true drink of moderation, for in this country, at least, more drunkenness is caused by beer and spirits than ever is caused by light table wines. This without even going into the undeniable fact that wine is healthier and less fattening than either of the other two products.

On balance it has been a good business, one with which I am happy and proud to have been associated.

Epilogue

Yes, it is over. But if anyone gets the impression that it was more trouble than it was worth, believe me it was not. We both have had fun, one helluva lot of fun, and if ever we had the chance we would do it all over again. But I have tried to convey the feeling that it was in no sense an escape. In the larger sense there is no escape from anything. Walden is an idealized concept that doesn't really exist, and even Thoreau probably came to recognize this at last.

So many people say, "But you escaped the boredom of the nine-to-five syndrome, and the tyranny and stupidity of the account executive and the program director." But I didn't "escape" them, I merely substituted the tyranny and stupidity of the Internal Revenue Service and the State Liquor Authority. Boredom? And isn't it boring to get up at five, fill the spray tank with a formulation you could make up in your sleep, mount the tractor, shove it into first gear and the accelerator into the fifth notch, and crawl down an alley of grapes that you have crawled down hundreds of times before?

The big difference is the reward. We were doing something we desperately wanted to do, and we were willing to put up with the tyrannies, the stupidities and the boredom to do it. We were doing something we considered important and meaningful, and this seldom happens on the nine-to-five shift. Are we happy, then, that we sold? Yes. It lifts our hearts to see new ground being turned, new vines being ordered, optimism everywhere. The creature that we created is alive and well.

But if there is one thing I want to do it is to take some of the romance out of what we both think is an already overromanticized occupation. Grape growing and winemaking are not for everyone. Many people are able to get their work done under the eye of a boss but do not have the discipline to organize their work and do it without someone breathing down their neck. This fact is being found out by many of today's young people who have left their jobs to go back to the soil, innocently believing that it will be no trick to grow all their own food, cut all their own fuel and weave all their own clothes. A few hardy souls have made it, but the great majority have thrown in the sponge. Nature is a tough taskmaster, far tougher than the most vitriolic of office managers.

But if after reading all the above there are those who have the youth, the strength, the capital and above all the unquenchable desire to be part of a culture and tradition that goes back to the roots of mankind, then by all means do it. There was a slim book written a few years ago called *The Man Who Made Wine,* which most perfectly describes the feeling of an aged winemaker on the eve of his retirement. The *maître de chai,* or cellarmaster, of a renowned Bordeaux winery, he had been given a dinner on his last night, and in his honor a bottle of each of the wines made during his tenure was opened. After the guests had gone the old man sat there alone, sampling his way back from the most recent vintage to the first. As the scent and the flavor of each bottle greeted him, the memorable events of that year unrolled before him. Good scenes, bad scenes, but sharply evoked and with great detail.

This is no more than the truth. When I open one of the rare bottles of our first vintage, 1953, I am immediately taken back to that first dedicated day, the small band of friends wearily coming down from the field with their last baskets, the worry of the first commercial fermentation, the ecstasy when all was well. And all the years sit there in their bottles, waiting to be lived again, for wine is not a creature of the moment and our good wines will last far longer than I will.

Yes, it was certainly fun, all of it. The uncertainties, the occasional failures, the rewards; the acclaim from the people whose opinions mattered—Jim Beard, Craig Claiborne, Poppy Cannon, Clementine Paddleford, Alexis Lichine, Frank Schoonmaker, Alec Waugh and many, many others. But even more than the acclaim was the sense of accomplishment, of doing something and doing it right, no compromise. Of making wine and making it from the juice of sound, ripe grapes, period.